the
Unfinancial
Planner

Joseph R. Simpson, CPA

www.theunfinancialplanner.com

PUBLISHER'S NOTE

This publication is designed to provide accurate and authoritative information in regard to the subject matter covered. It is sold with the understanding that the publisher is not engaged in rendering legal, financial, accounting or other professional service. If legal advice or other expert assistance is required, the service of a competent professional person should be sought.

Cypress Publishing Group, Inc.
11835 Roe # 187
Leawood, KS 66211
www.cypresspublishing.com

Library of Congress Cataloging-in-Publication Data

Simpson, Joseph R.
    The Unfinancial Planner / by Joseph R. Simpson
        p. cm.
    ISBN: 0-89447-335-2
    1.   Financial Planning – United States. 2. Personal
        Finance – United States. I. Title.
HF5386.A625 2002
658.02'2 – dc20

Printed in the United States of America

2002
10 9 8 7 6 5 4 3 2

To my wife Renee and
my daughter Amelia Ellen:
May life always be simple.
Love always.

Table of Contents

Let the Journey Begin

It seems that we all look at the world in just a little different light these days. There is a new appreciation and respect for the fragility of human existence and the value and importance of each and every day. Wouldn't it be nice if we could just spend all of our time in the company of friends and loved ones simply doing what makes us happy? The reality is that we have to get on with the business of living.

Let's face it; although our perspective may have changed, the bills didn't stop coming and we must still go to work on Monday morning. There are mortgage payments to make, credit card balances to pay off, education costs to lose sleep over and retirements for which to save. In fact, many of these realities have became even bigger concerns as we have helplessly watched our accumulated "fortunes" shrink before our eyes.

When it comes to personal finances, it is easy to give up and throw in the towel in difficult times like these. Will the glory days, when virtually anyone could strike it rich with little more than a modest bankroll and a brokerage account, ever return? Perhaps they will not. "Gold rushes" in any form are not all that common an occurrence.

That being said, as painful as this situation may be, it can be used as motivation to initiate positive change. I am a firm believer that in the long run people will generally make favorable changes in response to negative events and emotions. In fact, you will read later on how I have managed to channel the extreme power of negative thinking into positive action.

I know it's not easy to do, but you must look at this as an opportunity. Using the principles that appear on the following pages, you can begin to do just that. Do not lose hope or faith in the future. Instead, take positive action to improve every single day, making it better than each day before.

(Let Me Introduce Myself)

My name is Joe Simpson, and yes, I am a CPA. Sounds sort of like a confession, doesn't it? It seems that until recently no one cared too much about us or our profession. That was true until people realized that errors and omissions in financial statements can have a direct impact on their own wallet.

In case you were wondering, CPA stands for Certified Public Accountant. Green eyeshades, a pocket protector filled with retractable pencils, ties that are too skinny and glasses that are too thick are images that commonly come to mind. CPAs were traditionally thought to be many things, including honest, analytical, conservative, and most of all, boring! It's a stereotype well founded in American culture, and one we have done very little to help dispel. As a profession, our only recognizable claim to fame is that we count the ballots at the Academy Awards.

Most people think that we all do taxes and, worse yet, that we enjoy them. Not to worry, I despise taxes, as everything about them defies the concepts of simplicity that I hold so dear. Actually, CPAs are licensed and regulated "financial professionals" who generally hold degrees in accounting, have passed a difficult written examination to test our knowledge, and meet certain work experience requirements. You will find CPAs working in finance and accounting-related jobs in virtually every industry. Okay, I'm sure that's more than you ever wanted to know about us.

(In Search of the Comfort Zone)

Later in this book I'll discuss how setting short-term, achievable goals for yourself and turning the power of negative thinking into positive results can begin to move your life in a whole new direction. This book is living proof of both of those concepts in action.

One day about five years ago, I decided that if I was ever going to find a "comfort zone," a place where I could be relaxed, confident and secure in the future, I would need to put myself in control.

I therefore set a simple goal for myself. Find something that would allow me to channel my restless energy into action without incurring significant risk of failure. From that initial goal came the idea for writing a book.

I wrote a book outlining my philosophies on matters of personal finance, including the ideas and actions that have eventually helped to simplify my situation to the point where I was finally able to start turning it around. Believe me when I tell you, as difficult as it is to start, once you set those wheels of change in motion, they will continue to spin faster and faster until you decide to stop them.

(What This Book Is All About)

I'm afraid I do not have any magic potions or secret formulas to offer you. I can't tell you how to make the world a safer place or predict when the stock market could take off again. What I can give you is some good, solid, battle-tested advice on how to start removing the financial complexity from your life. Let me start by telling you about what this book is *not*.

It's not about making money or maximizing wealth. There will be no tips on picking stocks or refinancing your mortgage. There will be no tax savings schemes or advice on finding scholarships. I won't be teaching you how to invest in real estate with no money down or how to play the commodities markets.

If you're looking for a traditional book about personal finance or a "how to" guide, you've chosen the wrong one. This book is many things but traditional is not one of them. Simply put, this book is about keeping things SIMPLE.

(The Age of Complexity)

It has long been my observation that we humans do a very good job at complicating our lives. We do our best to convince ourselves that all this advancement and complexity is for the betterment of society. Although some advancement unquestionably is good, we now know all too well that progress does not always equate to improvement.

I am not suggesting that all progress has complicated our lives. In fact, I am perfectly happy using the microwave to heat up a cup of tea and have no desire to return to the days when you had to build a fire to make anything warm, including your-self. At some point, however, we crossed the line.

In the pages that follow I will help you to better understand and appreciate the power that money and finances can have on our lives. More importantly, I will teach you ways to minimize their impact, not so much in terms of dollars and cents but more so in terms of your time and emotions. With just a little change in perspective and a few simple ideas, you can begin pushing financial issues to the background, clearing the way to make some really important changes in your life.

(The Power of Simplicity)

Simplification is the key to change. Before you can fix some-thing you have to understand what's wrong. The simpler it is, the easier it is to find the problem. To move forward, you must make a commitment to simplify all aspects of your personal life. Strip away the complex analysis and replace it with good common sense and gut instinct. At the same time, learn to re-spect, understand and control your emotions.

For years, I made virtually all my decisions, financial and otherwise, based upon the conventional view of "right" and "wrong." When it comes to your finances, it's time to stop think-ing exclusively in terms of what everyone else thinks is right or wrong. The lesson I have learned about money is simple. There is no right or wrong way to manage it, only ways that work and ways that do not work *for you.* Control your money before it controls you. Don't let it become your reason to get up each day. Earn some, keep some, play with some, and give some away. Always keep it in perspective.

(Back to Basics)

It was easy to understand money principles as a small child. Put money inside your piggy bank, smash it open when it was full, count the money, go to the store, and buy what you want. Everything was so easy back then!

Well, as the years went by that basic principle that worked so well for us as kids seemed to get lost. Maybe it started when you landed your first job, perhaps babysitting or a paper route. Now all of a sudden, your piggy bank was insufficient, so you went to the bank and opened a savings account.

Gradually we moved farther and farther away from the concepts of simplicity embodied in that little bank. At some point, we discovered that you didn't really need to save money at all in order to buy things. Other people with piggy banks much bigger than yours, like banks and finance companies, will lend it to you.

That's right about the time when you enter what I call the "consumption phase" of personal financial development. It starts off innocently enough, as you acquire things like clothes, stereos, CDs and videos.

Eventually, you progress to bigger things like computers, houses, furniture and cars. Before you know it, you have credit card bills, a mortgage, home equity loans, personal loans, and a car payment to make.

The consumption phase is generally followed by the "accumulation phase," when you start looking to put your money away for the future.

You open up retirement accounts, including 401(k)s and IRAs; get a brokerage account or two; buy stocks and insurance; invest in mutual funds, certificates of deposit and money market accounts; and begin saving for college and retirement. You might prepare a detailed financial plan to help you manage this challenging phase of personal financial development. Before you know it, you will have become a full-fledged financial products consumer.

You get the idea. As time goes by, you move farther away from your simplistic beginnings. We all may be able to learn something from the simple, unsophisticated container filled with change that sat atop our dresser through the childhood years.

It wasn't technologically advanced or the least bit complex, but it served its purposes well. It makes a lot of sense for us, as a means of clarification and simplification, to sit back and consider how it was that something that used to be so simple got so complex.

(Psychology of Money)

Everyone has advice on how we can manage our money. Walk into your local bookstore, pick up the Sunday business section of your newspaper, read any of those personal finance magazines, or listen to talk radio, and you will find advice on managing your personal finances. Problem is, most of it simply is not that good, and it is not the kind of advice that you need.

Most financial advisors are more than happy to dish out traditional financial advice that may be 100% "reasonable and correct" from a bottom-line perspective.

Unfortunately, personal decisions about managing money should be 90% based on practical realities and only 10% based on bottom-line results. The advice that the traditional thinkers hand out is oftentimes based 90% upon bottom-line results and 10% upon practical realities. To make it worse, some advisors can be more interested in their own bottom line than in yours.

If you are ever going to achieve peace and simplicity in your personal financial situation, you must at times ignore the advice of the traditionalists and refuse to follow the herd. There would be no reason to write this book if all of my ideas were consistent with those of the other experts.

If you are to benefit from this book, you must free yourself from the traditional ways of thinking about personal finances. You must give priority to the left side of your brain once in a while, and do what will work for you, regardless of what others say is right or wrong.

Through my observations and experience, I have gained insight into many of the financial issues that people are concerned about and that cause them to worry. At the same time, I have seen that the vast majority of people have not figured out how to get from where they are now to where they want to be. At the other extreme, there are those who have identified the means but have so regimented themselves in trying to achieve their financial goals that all the fun of life is gone.

Most of us add more complexity to our lives than we need and have become too preoccupied with matters of personal finance. Whether it is by circumstance, by choice, or by poor decision, we have drifted into a situation that we never would have chosen if given the chance.

The constant marketing push of the financial services industry has some of us constantly balancing, forecasting, calculating and agonizing over money. Simplification requires more of a change of mind than it does a change of condition.

(The Complexity Quotient)

Before we go any farther, it is very useful to do an assessment of your family finances by calculating what I refer to as the "complexity quotient." Go ahead, put down the book and get a pencil and a piece of paper. Just answer these simple questions about your household and then add up your total.

1. How many bank credit cards do you currently have?
2. How many of them do you carry with you?
3. How many store credit cards do you have?
4. How many do you carry with you?
5. How many home equity lines/loans do you have now or have you had in the past?
6. How many bank accounts (checking, savings, etc.) do you have?
7. How many trips per week do you make to the ATM?
8. How many mutual funds do you own?
9. How many times have you moved money from one stock or mutual fund to another during the last 12 months?
10. How many times in the last year did you spend time on the Internet or elsewhere researching potential investments?

11. In your retirement/401(k) accounts, how many different investment options have you currently chosen?

12. In how many companies do you own stock?

13. How many times did you buy or sell shares within the past month?

14. How many different accounts do you have set up to pay for future education costs?

15. In how many dividend reinvestment plans do you participate?

16. How many brokerage (including Internet) accounts do you have?

17. How many bank certificates of deposit do you have?

18. How many checks do you write in an average month?

19. How many hours per month do you spend paying bills?

20. How many hours per month do you spend balancing your checkbook?

21. How many nights last month did you lie in bed thinking about something that had to do with money?

22. How many times have you refinanced your mortgage?

23. How many insurance policies do you have?

24. How many hours per month do you spend working on your budget?

25. How many times have you been to see a financial advisor or planner within the past year?

26. How many subscriptions do you have to personal finance magazines?

27. How many hours does it take you to gather the information needed to do your income tax?

28. How many forms are attached to your tax return?

Total your answers and you have what I refer to as your **"complexity quotient."** Don't put too much stock in the numerical results. The purpose of this exercise is really just to get you thinking about all the seemingly innocent little pieces of your financial life that individually may seem quite innocent but collectively may add up to one big mess.

So what's a "good" complexity quotient? It depends on what other factors you have in your life that contribute to your personal complexity, like being married, having children, both spouses working or owning a business. In general, if your complexity quotient is more than 150, then you've done a pretty fair job of complicating your financial life. Anything less than 50 is good.

(What It All Means)

Financial simplification involves much more than just the number of credit cards you have in your wallet or the frequency of your visits to the ATM. Our lives, financial and otherwise, are dramatically more complex than that.

Although simplification won't solve all of your problems, everyone can benefit from it, regardless of income, current financial condition, or whether or not your complexity quotient is high or low. Start by forcing yourself to take notice of all the little complexities you take for granted each day. For example, maybe you receive several bank, brokerage, mutual fund and retirement account statements, two or three insurance bills, and four or five credit card bills every month. Perhaps you spend a couple of hours every other week paying bills and another couple balancing the checkbook each month.

Make a concerted effort to pay attention to all these little things for a period of time. Whether it's that extra trip to the ATM or the 10 minutes you spend lying in bed thinking about an unpaid credit card bill, for one week make a mental note each and every time you think about or do something related to your money—that is, other than spend it. You will almost certainly be amazed at how large a part of your life your finances really consume.

Simplifying your life beyond the financial sphere is something that could make a real difference. At this point, such philosophical change may be well beyond the scope of this book.

Just be aware that changing your financial position and outlook may lead you to other changes, and the cumulative effect may be a much simpler, more rewarding lifestyle. Proceed to read this book with an open mind and remember that any step you make or action you take to render things less complex will almost certainly lead to improvement. Moving back a few steps on the path where you came from can help you move forward in directions you have never been.

We will start off slowly with some easy first steps you can take to help figure out where you are and how far you need to go. Gradually, we will work our way on to the more difficult principles, ones that will require you to adopt some really new ways of thinking. By the time you finish this book, you should question virtually every aspect of your personal finances. Hopefully along the way you will gain the courage to think outside the lines and challenge yourself to reject the status quo as you begin your journey back to simplicity.

(The Disclaimer)

Before we begin, there is one last matter of business to handle. Here is my disclaimer:

Please understand that the thoughts and ideas expressed in this book are those of the author. It includes suggestions for simplifying and improving life, financial and otherwise. These are only suggestions for simplification; they may not maximize wealth or optimize returns. In fact, some financial "experts" will assert that some of the ideas are downright ridiculous. There will be opposing opinions. However, our primary objective is to minimize the amount of time spent dealing with personal finance and maximize the amount of time spent doing the things that are really important in life. In other words, this book is all about quality of life and how to maximize it without shooting yourself in the foot financially.

Principle 1
Keep It Simple

The ultimate goal of financial simplification can only be realized if you can decrease the number of pieces in your personal financial puzzle. The first thing you will need to do in this regard is to get organized. You know—get control of all those documents, statements, bills, and papers that fill your mailbox, desk drawers, file cabinets, and kitchen countertop. Once that step is complete, you can turn your focus toward identifying ways to reduce and eliminate all this clutter.

Often people will spend enormous amounts of energy finding ways to deal with personal financial complication after it occurs. The real solution is to find ways to cut it off at the source, to prevent the problems from ever occurring.

(Finding the Pieces)

The first step in putting together any puzzle is to find all the pieces. To do this, starting today and continuing for one month, I want you to gather up every piece of non-junk mail that relates to your personal finances and throw it into a large box.

At the end of the month, the box will likely include credit card and utility bills; statements from your checking, savings, and money market accounts; auto loan and leases; money market and mutual funds; brokerage accounts; 401(k); IRAs; dividend reinvestment plans; 529 college savings plans; certificates of deposit, home equity, student and personal loan statements; doctor and dentist bills; correspondence from auto, life, homeowner and health insurance companies; tax-related items, etc.—you know, all the financial clutter that fills your mailbox every day.

Mix in loan payment coupon bonds, home equity line of credit checkbooks, savings bonds, pay stubs, ATM receipts, checks you write and receive, credit card receipts, and deposit and withdrawal slips. Remember, you are trying to find every single piece of your puzzle. Once you do, just chuck them in the box.

For dramatic effect, after one month, take the contents of that box and dump it all out on the kitchen table. Now stand back and look at what you have. What lies on the top of that table are all the pieces to your personal financial puzzle. For most people, it's simply one big mess!

(Your Appetite for Simplicity)

Before we go any farther, you need to ask yourself a question that requires an honest answer. Do you like the fact that your finances are complicated? There are many people who cannot honestly answer no when asked this question. They enjoy the complexity and rely on complication to keep things interesting and to keep them motivated. These are the same people who feel that anything easy is probably not worthwhile. Are you one of these people?

One sure sign that you could be the type of person who thrives on complexity is if you own and use a personal financial management software program like Quicken or Money. If so, ask yourself if you are using it simply because you think it can help or is it because deep down inside you really enjoy all the analysis of your financial affairs?

Some people just love to make things complicated, intentionally or unintentionally. They are the ones who will spend hours on the Internet searching for a perfect airline ticket they could have found with one 10-minute phone call. They subscribe to and read every issue of *Consumer Reports*. They look forward to going home every night and logging on the Internet just to find out how much their investment account balances have changed during the day. They have an insatiable appetite for information, and once they have access to it, they can easily become obsessed with analyzing it.

To help determine your appetite for complexity, consider this scenario. Let's say that you are having trouble with your clothes dryer and decide it's time to get a new one. If you spend the next four weeks comparison shopping at every appliance store in town, then you probably have a pretty strong appetite for complexity. You see needing a new dryer as an opportunity. If, however, you rush to the nearest Sears and buy the first one you look at, then you probably have very little appetite for complication. To you, having to buy a new dryer is just an unfortunate diversion and just another expenditure.

Most of us are somewhere in between these two propositions. We like to make reasonably informed decisions but have no desire to waste time with endless amounts of information and overly complex analysis.

Regardless of your appetite for complexity, anyone can benefit from simplification. Your financial puzzle must achieve the level of simplicity with which you are comfortable. If you like a little complexity, having a puzzle that is too easy will bore you. Similarly, if you have no appetite for complexity, you may easily give up on a difficult puzzle. The challenge is to find just the right balance that works for you.

(Designing a New Puzzle)

Now back to those puzzle pieces on your kitchen table. Let's assume you are looking to spend a bit less time putting your puzzle together and more time doing the things that are important to you. What do you do? You reduce the number of pieces of course. It's just common sense. The fewer the pieces, the easier it should be to put it together.

So, how do you go about reducing the complexity of a puzzle? One thing you should *not* do is indiscriminately start throwing away pieces. Missing pieces can make any puzzle far more complicated to put together. A better approach is to simply design an entirely new puzzle. That's right, start from scratch and design a new, easier puzzle, one with well-defined shapes and images and fewer pieces.

So, how do you redesign a new personal financial puzzle? Start by making an inventory list of the pieces to your current puzzle. Then just like when putting together the real thing, try dividing it up into broad sections, like "banking," "investments," "bills," "credit," "education," "retirement," "insurance," "house," "car," etc. Chances are that each section of your puzzle will be made up of several pieces.

Once you are done listing the sections and finding all the relevant pieces, sit back and look at each one with an objective mind. That is, throw your predetermined bias out the window. Remember your goal is to find ways to simplify your puzzle and reduce the number of pieces.

(Change in Attitude)

Using the concepts embodied in these principles, you will find many opportunities to simplify your puzzle. In some cases, it may be something as easy as combining accounts, like bringing your mutual funds, 401(k) balances from previous employers, brokerage activities, checking accounts, savings, money market accounts, CDs, and IRAs together at one or two financial institutions or just cutting up and cancelling old credit cards. In other cases, it may be much more difficult, requiring that you adopt an entirely new perspective on some very traditional issues, like paying for college, buying a house or saving for retirement.

Each piece may seem insignificant in and of itself, but when combined, they can create one big problem. Opportunities for simplification are everywhere but are not always plainly obvious. For example, you might consolidate your local, long distance and even cellular phone service into one provider. Consider high-speed cable Internet access and get rid of extra phone lines and multiple Internet service providers, receiving just one bill for cable TV and Internet service.

Get rid of all those e-mail accounts and start using just one. Eliminate all those extra entries in your checkbook by cutting up your debit card. Consolidate your insurance policies to save time and money. These little things may not seem important, but every one contributes to complexity.

In some instances, simplification will not come without a general change in your attitude, requiring that you start to think in simpler terms. Let's take investments as an example. We have all heard about the benefits of diversification. However, at some point, you can go too far. People can take diversification to an extreme and any benefit they derive may be more than offset by the added complication it brings.

How many individual mutual funds do you have? You could diversify simply by investing in different funds at one or two mutual fund companies rather than multiple accounts at different companies. In addition, if you own several mutual funds, chances are that they may be investing in many of the same stocks anyway.

If it's diversification of your equity portfolio you seek, you will read in principle 16 that it's possible to achieve this by buying single shares in Exchange Traded Funds rather than owning individual shares in many companies. At the same time, you can gain more control over your tax liabilities and simplify your tax return.

You can now get most of the financial products and services that you will ever need (from traditional deposits, loans, and credit cards to insurance, investments, and brokerage services) right at your local bank. When combined with excellent, user-friendly Web sites and Internet banking services like those offered by HSBC Bank USA at www.us.hsbc.com, these institutions offer a tremendous opportunity for consolidation.

In addition, many companies now offer consolidated statements that will combine all of your accounts in a single, monthly summary. Take advantage of these services and gravitate your business toward those who offer it.

You need to take every single piece of that puzzle on the table and honestly ask yourself, "Do I really need it?" There are plenty of opportunities to reduce the number of pieces if you just look hard enough and let yourself be a little creative.

(Every Piece Counts)

It's very easy for personal finances to get out of control over time. An account here, an investment there — in isolation, they all seem so innocent. Before you know it, however, you can have a big, complicated puzzle on your hands, and all the pieces start to look the same.

It's far easier to attack a little problem before it becomes a big problem. Don't make the mistakes that so many individuals and businesses make every day. Step by step, they lead themselves down the road to complexity. It is not until problems surface that they stop and assess what they have done to themselves, often concluding that it's too late to turn the situation around.

Principle 2
Get Organized

Try to imagine an automobile assembly plant where the parts are scattered all over the factory. Need a steering wheel? "Check in the paint shop, I think I saw some there," the foreman tells the assembly worker. "Windshields are over by tailpipes, but be careful, those may be the old ones that don't fit anymore. While you're over there, see if you can find any tires." Chaos would surely result.

As outrageous as this seems, many of us control our personal financial affairs in a manner not too different from what I have just described. It seems that the discipline that we have to keep things running smoothly at our jobs can be all but lost once we enter the comfort of our own personal lives.

It's amazing how much you can improve things with just a little order. Think about how much time you spend each month chasing and managing paperwork. Whether it's sorting through the mail, paying bills, entering transactions in and balancing your checkbook, or just filing things away, it takes a lot of time and energy to stay on top of it all.

(The Order of Chaos)

At one time, I was truly out of control. There were stacks and stacks of papers all over the house. I couldn't find anything! Whether it was a copy of the instruction book for the VCR, a property tax receipt, the registration papers for my car, or my health insurance card, if I needed it, chances were pretty good that I was going to have to search for it.

Then one day, I realized that if I was ever going to be able to figure out how to simplify my life, I first needed to know how complicated I had made it. I decided the only way to do that was to get organized.

It's one of the easiest and most beneficial things you will ever do. When you get done, you will feel wonderful. You don't need to invest in any fancy filing system or sophisticated software either. In fact all you need to do is:

- Get a couple of big (2ft X 2ft) file boxes, 8-10 accordion-style file folders, and one magic marker.

- Using the marker, label the folders as follows: "Car," "Credit," "House," "Important Papers," "Insurance," "Investments," "Job," "Purchases," "Medical and Dental," and "Taxes."

- Every time a document arrives, categorize it into one of the folders and file it away.

- Once a year, go through the box to see what can be thrown away.

- Keep only the papers that you need from year to year.

That's really all there is to it. With four steps you can gain complete control over every important piece of paper you may ever need. You will be amazed at how much better you feel about things once you get them organized and how much time you will save when you can easily find any important paper.

Here is a brief summary of some of the types of documents that you may wish to include in each folder:

AUTO

Bill of sale, registration papers, loan and lease agreements, warranties, and repair bills. Don't save receipts for gas and washes unless you have a business or must substantiate them for taxes.

CREDIT

The envelopes and inserts that new credit cards are shipped in that indicate your account number and the issuer's phone number, extra credit cards, copies of loan applications or agreements, line of credit or home equity checkbooks, credit reports. Keep your paid credit card bills here.

HOUSE

Property deed, search and survey, mortgage note, title documents, copies of tax bills, receipts for any significant improvements.

IMPORTANT PAPERS

Note: You may want to put this file in a fireproof box.

Birth certificates, marriage licenses, voter registration cards, passports, Social Security cards, college diplomas.

INSURANCE

Copies of life, auto, disability, umbrella and health policies along with spare insurance cards.

INVESTMENTS

Copies of your latest brokerage, mutual fund, IRAs, 401(k)s, stock purchase and option plans, savings account, and money market account statements, as well as account documentation and stock certificates that you hold.

JOBS

Employee benefit elections and coverages, stock option plan certificates, pension plan and Social Security information, union papers, employee tax withholding certificates (W-4), copies of evaluations, and important letters and communication.

Basically, anything you may need to keep related to your job that you might not want to keep filed at your desk.

PURCHASES

Receipts and warranty information on all major purchases. Also, if it's something that was installed, remember to write on the warranty card the name of the installer.

MEDICAL

Benefit and coverage information, copies of medical and dental bills, insurance reimbursement notifications, and important medical test results.

TAXES

Old tax returns along with all relevant forms including W-2s, 1099s, receipts for charitable contributions, mortgage statements, current year tax forms, receipts, statements, and any other document you will need at tax time to do your return.

DO NOT create a file labeled "Miscellaneous." It's just an invitation to keep things you really don't need.

(File Management)

Once you put a filing system in place, there are two keys to keeping it up and running smoothly. First, don't try to save too much. Most folks keep way more than they need. Second, don't let the filing pile up on you. Stay on top of it. The bigger you let the pile of papers get, the less likely it is that you're going to want to deal with it.

One thing that works for me is keeping a small box where I sort the mail. If you know a piece of paper is destined for your files, put it there and then make sure you empty that box at least once every other week or so and file the papers.

Tailor the files to your requirements. For example, you might need one labeled "College" for student loan applications, grants, financial aid forms, tuition bills, etc. If you build a new house, you will certainly need a "Construction" file. The object is to have a place ready and available to store every document that you want and need to keep and to eliminate the piles of envelopes stacked on the kitchen countertop and papers stuck inside the telephone book.

(Clean Up After Yourself)

Don't forget to go through your files and clean them out at least once a year. Always be looking for ways to reduce or eliminate what you are saving.

Organizing your files may not seem like much, but it is a major step toward simplification. Once you get things organized you can really start assessing how disorganized you actually are. Organization also serves another important purpose. It forces you to inventory yourself.

Try figuring your complexity quotient again (based on the questions on pages 15 and 16) once you finish organizing your documents. After you have found everything, your complexity number will almost certainly be higher.

(Throw It Out)

When it came to managing paperwork, I was once truly out of control. As I look at it now, it is hard to believe some of the completely ridiculous things I was doing.

For example, like many people I would take paid electric, phone, water, gas, insurance, cable, and cellular bills and put them in a box to save presumably forever. I also kept boxes and boxes of statements from checking accounts, savings accounts, mutual funds, credit cards, 401(k)s, brokerage accounts, etc. I even kept receipts from ATM transactions, credit card purchases, direct debits, deposits, direct deposits, and an endless supply of payroll stubs.

Since most of us have been trained since birth that it is generally better to save than it is to throw away, it's very easy to become a compulsive saver, overwhelmed in this endless supply of paperwork and information we must manage as adults.

(To Have and to Hold)

At some point, most folks just give up even trying to figure out what they should keep or throw away and just decide to keep everything.

If you have difficulty letting go, try a little experiment. Write down the following two questions. Before making a final decision to hold any single piece of paper, ask yourself:

1. Do I really need it — not do I *want* it, but do I really need it? Don't fall into the old trap of "I might want that one day."

2. What are the consequences of not having it?

The first question will be far more difficult to answer than the latter. That's because compulsive savers may have already convinced themselves that whatever it is that they are saving "needs" to be kept.

This won't be easy, especially if you are trying to break a pattern of past abuse. Take those electric bills you saved from last year. Do you really need them? Chances are that you have never gone back to look up something on an old electric or utility bill. If you have, it was probably information you could have easily obtained from the utility company.

What are the consequences of not having those old electric bills? Well, the Public Service Commission could rule that your electric company has been overcharging residential customers for the past 20 years and that if you can produce copies of every bill you paid you could be entitled to a $10,000 refund! Okay, that may be possible, but it's not likely.

Furthermore, chances are that if this did happen, the calculation of your refund would be based on the records maintained by the utility company and not your own. "Fine, but how can I verify the calculation if I don't have my own records?" Well, you can ask that copies of the bills be provided to you. "What if they can't do that?"

At this point you are at the third level of possible reasons for holding on to that paid bill. "What if I am entitled to a refund; what if they can't get copies of my bills; what if they screw up the calculation?" The reason for saving that piece of paper has now moved far beyond the reasonable, and the answer is obvious. Throw out the utility bills! "But it's just one tiny piece of paper, and I don't see what harm it does to keep it." In and of itself, keeping one piece of paper is fairly harmless.

However, keeping a piece of paper that you really have a low probability of ever needing is symptomatic of a deeper problem. Soon you will have a pile of paper, then several piles of paper, and before long, you won't be able to easily segregate the really important ones from the ones that are not important at all.

Pay stubs are another good example of keeping records for no reason. Why do you need them after you receive your annual W-2 or better yet, why do you need them at all? There are probably some people who actually add them up and compare them to their year-end W-2, but I for one have never had a reason to go back to an old pay stub for any reason.

How about credit card receipts for routine purchases? Maybe you keep them to agree the charges to your monthly statement. That's fine, but unless it's for something you might want to return or may need for tax purposes, get rid of them.

Many companies now send you summarized annual statements for accounts such as brokerage, mutual funds, credit cards, and even utilities. All the information you have in the monthly statements is contained within those annual statements. So what do most people do? Why, they save both the monthly and the annual statements of course! Ask yourself the two questions from page 29, and you quickly realize that once you get the annual statement there is no need to keep the monthly ones.

(E-Files)

You may also find that much of the information you need or think you needed from that pile of documents is now available online. With the increasing availability of account information through the Internet, it has become even easier to make the decision to toss things away that you once felt compelled to keep.

Online bank accounts can give you instant access to your balance or recent and even historical transactions. They contain search mechanisms that allow you to look for certain transactions by dollar amount, payee, and otherwise.

Online brokerage accounts give you instant access to the purchase and sales price for securities transactions, dividend information, and stock splits. Credit card companies give you up-to-date balance and transaction information, all of which you kept hard copies of in the past.

There are some documents like W-2s, 1099s, and receipts for charitable contributions needed to prepare your tax return that you are going to have to keep. Once you have gained control over all your documents, however, it will be far easier for you to spot the essential ones and focus your attention on saving the things that you really do need to keep. Remember, if it isn't important enough to fit into one of your document files, then it's probably not important enough to keep.

(Checks and Balances)

For as long as I can remember, my bank sent canceled checks back to me along with my account statement. What did I do with them? I saved them of course because I thought I needed them. Why else would the bank send them?

A few years back, my bank decided that they were spending way too much time and money getting all those checks back to customers. They asked themselves, "Do customers really need them?" Their answer was a resounding no, and I stopped getting my checks back. In time, I too realized that I didn't need them. On the rare occasion that I might actually need to produce a copy of a canceled check, I just call my bank on the phone or order the copy online.

Similarly to how my bank conditioned me to accept a major change in the documentation they were providing, you too will have to condition yourself to change what you consider to be the acceptable level of documentation that you need to maintain.

(Yes You Can)

To ease the transition and the emotional stress you are likely to endure, I suggest that you go out and buy yourself a nice new trashcan. If you find yourself making a decision to throw away something that you used to keep but are still not 100% convinced that it's the right thing to do, toss it in that new trash can rather than throwing it away completely. This way you will know it is safe and secure should you need to get it.

Chances are that you will have no need to retrieve anything out of that receptacle. After about six months, analyze how you did. If you never went into the trashcan during that period, the decision has been made for you. There is no need to save anything you put into it. If you did go into the trashcan, make sure you write down why. If the reason is legitimate, then save the document.

Learning how to manage and control the clutter in your personal financial life is a key step toward achieving financial simplicity. You must condition yourself to change your immediate reaction from "save it" to "throw it away." Once this mindset firmly takes hold, you will quickly be able to spot the important documents from the unimportant ones. An organized filing system is the foundation upon which to begin assembling your new financial puzzle.

Principle 3

Make Your Computer Work for You

No book that deals with complexity would be complete without reference to personal computers. I'll admit that I was a very slow convert to the information age. I have a lot of this to blame on timing.

You see, when I was in college, an apple was something you ate and a notebook was something in which you wrote. We actually still used typewriters. Remember those things?

Just as I was leaving college, the personal computer was beginning to launch itself headfirst into society. Since I was pre-occupied with other things at the time, I barely noticed. Just a few years after my graduation, however, personal computers would become as commonplace in offices as adding machines, and the typewriter would be all but replaced.

For many, the personal computer began as something they were forced to deal with at work, but in their personal life it was a novelty they could do without. That is, until the 1990s when the Internet exploded. Suddenly, the computer had a whole different and expanded role in the average person's life.

(Cyber Pay)

It was the Internet-based electronic bill-paying service that my bank offered me a year or so ago that changed my opinion of the personal computer and the Internet forever. There have been few things in my lifetime that have contributed so much to the simplification of my personal financial life as the Internet banking service that I use at www.us.hsbc.com. If you are not already a convert to these services, don't be intimidated. You will be amazed at how easy it can be to set up and use. Once you get started, there will be no reason to ever turn back, and you will wonder how you ever paid bills before. Not only will you be able to cut a significant amount of time from your monthly bill-paying routine, you will also have immediate access to all of you account information, including loans, deposits, CDs, and even your brokerage account. It even allows you to keep an electronic checkbook.

Through my bank's Web site, I set up virtually everyone I used to write checks to as electronic "payees" on my checking account. Then, with a few clicks of the mouse, I simply tell my bank when and how much I want to pay them, and they do the rest automatically.

I have always been of the opinion that the old-fashioned checkbook is pretty darn easy to use and at first could think of no good reason to pay my bills in any other way. However, paying bills the old-fashioned way means sifting through piles of envelops, writing checks, entering them in the register, addressing envelopes, buying stamps, and mailing. It is time consuming and expensive.

Now, I simply take the bills right from my mailbox, turn on the computer, click on the appropriate electronic payee, enter the amount of the payment and the date it is due, and I'm done. Better yet, I can throw away the "paid" bills immediately rather than piling them up on the kitchen counter. They even have a check register built in so I don't even have to write them down anymore. All the information I would ever need about my bills is neatly stored away in the bank's computer, accessible at any time.

No more running out of checks, waiting in lines at the post office for stamps, or tearing off those annoying little flaps on return envelopes. Electronic bill paying transfers much of the complexity of this burdensome process from you to your bank, and much to my amazement, it can really simplify your life and free up a significant amount of time.

As much as I am a convert to Internet banking and bill paying, you must be cautious so as to protect yourself from errors. There are a few things you need to watch out for:

- If you do not rely upon an electronic checkbook, make sure you remember to enter the e-pay amount in your checkbook. It's easy to forget to do it.

- It's very easy to make a mistake when you first set up the payees. You might enter an address incorrectly or transpose numbers in your account. Check very closely the first time you use it to make sure the payments are being properly credited.

- The fees are relatively small now as banks try to get you hooked, but they may start creeping up on you. Look for any "relationship" packages at the bank that holds your mortgage. They may throw in Internet banking for free.

You don't need more than one of these services either. It seems everyone wants you to access your accounts online and make payments to them directly. You can do without that extra complication. Setting up electronic access to many different accounts just so you can pay them online is unnecessary. One Internet bill-paying service from your local bank is all you need to get the job done.

(Perpetual Complexity)

The personal computer and the Internet are undoubtedly two of the most significant technological innovations of our generation. Nothing has ever brought such sweeping and revolutionary change to our society in such a short period of time. Computers and the Internet have changed our homes, our offices and our world in ways that one could never have imagined even a few short years ago.

For all the wonderful things computers have brought to our lives, it's easy to overlook the negatives. Think about it. Is your life easier today than it was before the advent of the computer? Sure, there are some things like Internet bill paying that save time and money, and word processing software beats the heck out of the typewriter.

For all the good things the computer has brought, there are an abundance of negatives that go along with it. Take shopping for example. Is it any easier or cheaper to buy things over the Internet than it is to go to a store? You may not need to look for a parking space or deal with an unfriendly sales clerk, but you must contend with many inconveniences including unfriendly site designs, complicated and time-consuming order and billing forms, shipping charges, and complicated returns. On top of that, it's not nearly as much fun as browsing at the local mall.

E-mail is another example. We have a wonderfully sophisticated e-mail system at our office that has made communication between co-workers and the outside world incredibly efficient and effective. The problem is, however, that it's too darn efficient and effective.

I spend the better part of each day opening, reading, sorting, filing, deleting and passing off to other e-mail boxes the hundreds of documents that come to me. These are not just ordinary documents either, but documents attached to documents, which are attached to other documents, which are attached to spreadsheets, which are attached to files, and on and on and on.

What did we do before e-mail? We communicated with each other by phone, fax and, believe it or not, in person. Are we all that more productive now than we were before the advent of e-mail? Maybe, but in many cases we may actually be less productive.

When it wasn't so easy to communicate, we took a little more time to think about what we were doing before we did it. Now it's all so mindless. When something arrives in electronic form, my first inclination is to get rid of it by passing it to someone else. E-mail makes it easy to do so. No thought required, just the click of a few keys and it's gone.

(Information Age)

One of the biggest negatives associated with computers and the Internet may also be one of its biggest positives. We now have access to much more information than we ever had before. It's this abundance of information that may be serving to complicate our lives in ways we never thought possible. We just may know too much!

A few years back when I was desperately searching to simplify my life, I stopped reading the daily newspaper and watching television news programs. I came to realize that both were giving me far more information each day than I actually needed.

You may believe this was just a form of the "ostrich approach." That is, I put my head in the sand and hope it all goes away. However, it really wasn't that at all. Rather, I simply asked myself if I really needed to have all this information, most of it depressing, about things that will probably have little or no impact on my life.

Just as cutting down the number of different bank accounts you have and credit cards you carry can lead to simplification, so too can cutting down on the amount of information you have to deal with each day. The computer and the Internet give us more information than we can possibly use. The problem is that many of us try to use every bit of it.

(Travel Pains)

Before the Internet, if you wanted to make an airline reservation you picked up the phone and called a travel agent or the airline directly to check fares and schedules. Now when you want to book a flight reservation, you conduct an exhaustive search by best route, the lowest fare and maybe even the type of airplane on which you want to fly. You can even bid the price you want to pay!

Remember when planning a vacation meant looking over those nice glossy brochures you picked up from the travel agent? Now you can spend hours searching on the Internet for the best possible hotel at the lowest possible price. You plan your activities, find restaurants, book your rental car and check weather forecasts all from your keyboard. Why do we do it?

Instant access to all the information is what makes it possible. Was it really so bad when you didn't have all that information? Probably not, in fact it was probably much easier than it is today.

(Take Stock)

Stocks are another good example. Before the Internet, most people bought stocks based on recommendations from brokers or friends, articles or news stories they read, or because they used a product or service sold by the company.

You may have even obtained a copy of a recent financial statement or even went so far as to go to the library to get a Moody's report before you decided to purchase. Now, look on one of the sites devoted to stock trading or personal finance and you will find all the information you ever wanted to know about virtually any publicly traded company. You can even get instant access to filings with the Securities and Exchange Commission.

However, in this as in many things, some caution is necessary. Be sure that you are visiting reputable sites, at least ones that are linked from the major brokerages or from reputable organizations or news sources, like those you will find at www.cbsmarketwatch.com.

For those people who buy stocks, thanks to the Internet, they can now do so based upon their own research. They look at analysts' recommendations, insider trading, and pour over financial ratios and statistics. They monitor all the latest news developments and watch for industry trends. Investors obsessed with information can now get as much of it as they need.

(Information Management)

Is it necessarily bad to have all this information? Of course it's not. In the pages of this book, I have referenced many Internet sites that provide valuable and useful information. You just have to learn how to control all this information to prevent overload, or you may end up complicating things even more than before you had access to all this extra knowledge and you won't necessarily make better investments either.

Computers and the Internet have also served to take some of the spontaneity and fun out of what we do. I remember when I was a kid traveling with my parents, how exciting it was to stay in a hotel we had never seen before. Now thanks to the Internet, you can see it as many times as you would like before you arrive, at eight different angles, maybe even in live action streaming video from the "hotel cam."

There was a certain excitement associated with the lack of complete knowledge. Certainly it's good to be organized and prepared, but the computer has allowed us to go too far.

Like many things in life, computers and the Internet must be used in moderation. Handled properly they can provide you with just the right amount of information needed to complement your efforts at simplification. Used improperly they may result in confusion and distress. A computer is a powerful instrument of technology. Use it with the utmost of caution.

Principle 4

Control and Use Your Credit Cards

Take your wallet out right now and open it up. How many credit cards are in there? If you are like most people, you probably carry three to six cards with you all the time. Now, what's wrong with that? First, let's take the obvious. If you lose your wallet you have to cancel all those cards — that is if you actually remember which ones you were carrying.

More importantly it is an indication that you have over-complicated things. There may be reasons why you have more than one credit card. Your company may make you carry one for work-related expenditures. That's fine but explain the rest.

(Lost in the Maze)

You started out with just one card but as time goes by, your credit portfolio builds. Walking through your favorite department store you spot a leather coat that you absolutely must have. The salesperson asks, "Would you like to save an additional 10% on your purchase today?" Sure, all you have to do is sign up for a new credit card. It takes only a few minutes.

So you leave the store with a new coat and your new credit card. Not bad! Before you know it, five or six other department stores have signed you up in exchange for some one-time discount, free merchandise or attractive offer like deferred billing or interest-free financing. These department store cards are pretty much losers all the way around. Not only are they expensive, with interest rates generally running 20% or higher, they clutter your mailbox with account statements, complicate bill paying and worst of all, they tempt you into buying more. Many stores offer extra discounts or cash bonuses if you buy things using their card. Don't get drawn in.

(All the Credit You Will Ever Need)

Once you have established credit, the offers really start pouring in for new cards. Maybe it's the promise of a "2.99% introductory rate" or perhaps a "low, low 9.99% fixed rate" that tempts you to open the "invitation to apply." Along the way you decide to accept a card or two that gives you reward points that you can redeem for merchandise, cash rebates, frequent flier miles or rebates on new car purchases.

Then there was your first gold card. You couldn't pass that one up, especially with all the benefits including travel accident insurance, collision damage waiver, purchase protection and more. Before you know it, your wallet is bursting at the seams with plastic and your mailbox is full of bills. You may not even know how many credit cards you actually have.

(Take an Inventory)

Inventory each and every credit card you have, even if you don't use it. While you're at it, write down the issuer, card number and expiration date, the names appearing on the cards and the customer service number from the back of the card and place this information in your "Credit" file, which you created in principle 2. This information may come in handy some day.

Once you've done this, I want you to pick up each card one by one and ask yourself, "Why do I have it?" If your answer is any one of the following, then you have a great opportunity to simplify by getting rid of unnecessary cards:

- I liked the perks (free miles, cash back, rebates, or points).
- I received something for free or got a discount.
- There is no fee.
- It's affiliated with a cause I support (a school or charity).
- The interest rate was too low to pass up.
- I took advantage of a balance transfer option.
- It was sent when I bought something on deferred billing.
- By having more than one card, I can spread my spending out so that any one bill is not too overwhelming.

These reasons may offer sufficient justification to have any one of these credit cards, but if you have more than one of these cards for any of these reasons, you have a great opportunity to begin simplifying.

(The Perks)

I don't have to tell you that there are many credit cards out there that offer some terrific benefits. Regardless, many of the benefits that seem good when we sign our name to the application are never actually used.

Take purchase protection for example. It's really terrific that you can double the manufacturer warranty on major purchases by using your credit card to pay for it. However, most people will never qualify or bother to make a claim on the extended warranty as they lose the receipt, forget they have the protection or just decide that the hassles of trying to collect are not worth it.

Many of those perks are also supplemental to protection that already exists. Take, for example, lost baggage insurance. When is the last time you actually lost (permanently) a piece of luggage? Even if you have lost luggage or ever do, the airline may already cover most of the replacement cost.

Rental car insurance works basically the same way. Your personal auto insurance probably covers you in a rental car. Call and check with your insurance company. Don't think Mastercard is about to cut a check for $10,000 if you total the rental car. Your auto insurance is first in line whether you want it to be or not.

How about the "stuff" they offer like neat looking little calculators and telephones? Most of them are of such poor quality that they are seldom used. Same thing goes for the free miles they give you or points that you earn. Many of them never get redeemed or offer little value.

For example, say you need to spend $20,000 on your credit card to accumulate enough frequent flier miles for a round-trip ticket to Florida. You could have racked up the same $20,000 in purchases on a card that paid you a 1% cash rebate. Since the airline ticket could have been purchased for $189, you would have been better off using the cash back card instead. Since your purchasing power is limited, no matter how good a credit card looks, there is just not enough spending available to take full advantage of all those wonderful offers.

(Two Cards Are Better Than One)

It doesn't matter how many cards you currently have or the reasons why you have them; you can take a simple step that will greatly reduce the complexity of your credit situation. My advice is to get rid of all of your credit cards...except two! That's right, all but two should go. When I say get rid of them, I mean really get rid of them. Look at the customer service number on the back of the card, dial it up, and tell them to cancel the card immediately. Unused lines of credit on old cards are counted just like outstanding balances when you are applying for a loan.

Why keep two cards you ask? If you pay off your balance each and every month, then you may need only one. If, however, you are not inclined to pay the balance in full all the time, against the good advice of all traditional financial advisors I might add, two is the answer. One card I call your "convenience" card, and the other is your "financing" card. Use your convenience card to buy things and your financing card, if you must, to pay for or finance things.

So how do you choose a convenience card? Given the range of credit card offers out there today, no one should carry a single card that charges a fee or does not provide some benefit. For your convenience card, pick one that offers something that appeals to you like cash back, reward points, a rebate toward the purchase of a car, discounts, or donations made to your favorite charity. Use the Internet to shop around and find the card that works best for you.

Look solely at "big" benefits, the free stuff they use to market the card. Avoid cards that offer nothing more than a picture of your favorite sports team or race car.

You will quickly realize that accumulating all your charges on a single card will bring the benefits home quicker than chasing rewards on several cards at the same time. Just be careful not to put more on your convenience card than you are prepared to pay off each month, as credit card companies do charge you interest from the day a purchase is made unless the balance is paid in full. That is, there is no grace period on new purchases unless you have a zero balance each month.

If you are unfortunate enough to have to carry balances, you will need a second card. The choice of this financing card should be based entirely on the interest rate. Of course, the credit line will also have to be sufficient. Again, use the Internet to find the lowest rates and monitor those offers that show up in your mailbox. Remember, there is no need to ever carry a card that charges an annual fee.

(Juggling Act)

Contrary to popular belief it's not automatically a problem if you carry a balance on a credit card. In fact, if you manage your financing card properly by taking advantage of introductory rate offers, credit card financing can be one of the most affordable forms of borrowing you have. A word of caution, however: Moving balances from one financing card to another may make financial sense, but it surely will not simplify your life.

Unfortunately for many people, transferring balances is a reality they must deal with or resign to paying outrageous interest charges. If you find yourself in a position where you need to carry a modest balance on your financing card, find one with no annual fee and a low fixed rate and stick with it.

If your balance is large enough to justify juggling and you opt for one of those low introductory rate offers, immediately get yourself a nice BIG calendar, preferably one you look at every day. Find out the date the introductory rate expires, take a magic marker and in bold letters write yourself a note that says "pay off credit card" on the calendar two weeks before.

Write the payment mailing address and account number right on the calendar. You see, credit card companies are good at telling you about low rate introductory offers but not really good at letting you know when those offers expire.

Don't be late with a payment. Oftentimes, a late payment immediately bumps your introductory rate up to the current rate. Also, never mix your convenience charges and your financed balances. Unless you instruct them otherwise, the credit card company will apply your payments against the low-rate transferred balance first. So, if you're mixing new charges with old balances, you may be paying down the old balance and paying for the new charges at a higher rate.

Once you have taken full advantage of the low-rate period, don't make the mistake of keeping the card. Get rid of it! Call up the customer service representative, cancel it and cut it up. If necessary, take advantage of another low-rate offer or better yet, consider spending less money! I know that this is often easier said than done. Just remember, you must strive to never have more than two cards at any one time.

(Same as Cash)

You may also feel tempted to take advantage of those "no interest for six months" or "90 days same as cash" financing offers. Just remember that many of these offers are simply gimmicks to get you to open a credit account and force you to buy more expensive goods, as the cost of those interest-free periods is often passed on to the store resulting in higher prices. If you are considering one, there are pitfalls to watch out for and keep in mind.

Most of those interest-free agreements require you to make payment in full by a certain date, and if you don't, interest is charged on the full balance for the entire period it was outstanding. Similarly, these offers can automatically cancel if you make even one late payment.

I know these are tempting options and if managed properly can save you money, but they will not make your life any

simpler. It can be a lot of work managing these accounts, especially if you have more than one. Always remember to give
yourself a great big reminder of when the payment is due or
the introductory rate period expires. When it does, pay off the
balance, immediately cancel the account, and if they sent you a
credit card, tear it up.

(The Results)

If you can get down to just two credit cards you will begin
to reap the benefits of this important, easy step toward simplification almost immediately. Your mailbox will be less cluttered,
and your bill paying will be easier. With only two cards to keep
track of, it will be much easier to get those payments in on time
and avoid the astronomical late charges. In addition, your wallet will get a whole lot slimmer.

If you need help finding a low-interest credit card or sorting
through the perks, try a site like www.cardweb.com. Remember
that a credit card is a financial product and some thought and
homework should go into selecting one. Do a little homework,
compare the benefits, and make an informed decision.

(Track Your Spending)

As you will read later on, I hate budgets. That being said, I
cannot dispute the value of knowing where you spend your
money. If there were only a simple way to track your expenditures in a neat and orderly fashion without having to go though
the hassles of collecting and organizing mountains of paperwork! Well there is, and the answer is probably right in your
wallet.

Use your "convenience" card for all your normal purchasing activity and pay the balance off in full each month. When I
say you should use this card to pay for "all" your normal purchasing activity I do mean "all" of it.

There are very few places these days where your credit card
cannot be used. From gasoline and groceries, to stamps, movie

rentals and even some fast food places, you can buy just about anything with your convenience card.

If you follow this advice you will soon find that:

- Trips to the ATM are far less frequent.

- You are writing fewer personal checks, which can be a major hassle.

- You are less concerned about security (as you will need to carry very little cash).

- You will spend less time balancing your checkbook.

- There will be extra money in the checking account.

Let me caution you about the last one. Beware of all that extra money you have in your checking account. It's only an illusion. You don't have any more money. It only seems that way since you're not stopping at the ATM, writing checks or using your debit card every day.

The key to this principle is not only that you "buy" everything with your credit card but also that you "pay" for nothing with it! That means no compromises. This is your convenience card. You must be disciplined enough to pay off the balance on this card in full each and every month.

(Record Spending)

Aside from the convenience and the time you will save using your credit card for all your purchasing activity, the best part about it is that you will automatically have a quick and easy record of all of your spending activities, especially all those little things that are so easy to loose track of and tend to add up quickly. You know, like the $60 you took out of the ATM on Monday that is completely gone by Wednesday and you have no idea what you spent it on.

When you use your convenience card, all of your purchases are nicely organized on the single monthly statement delivered right to your mailbox.

Credit cards offer some distinct advantages over cash and can be an especially useful tool if you are trying to get control of your spending. By using your convenience card regularly, your check register and your monthly credit card statement will provide you with basically all the information you need to figure out where your money goes.

So stop all that sifting through endless piles of receipts. Simply grab a pencil and your monthly credit card statement. Go through each individual charge and place a letter next to it corresponding to the type of expenditure that you made.

For example, you could use "G" for groceries and household supplies; "E" for entertainment-related expenditures like movie rentals, concerts, sporting events and weekend getaways; "A" for automobile-related expenditures like gasoline, oil changes and car washes; and "D" for dining out.

Create as many categories as you want to fit your specific spending habits. Then all you need to do to figure out where the money was spent is to add it all up.

Go through your check register to pick up everything else you don't pay for with a credit card, categorize it, and you have instant analysis of your spending habits. What used to take hours can now be done in minutes.

(Debit Card Dilemma)

One relatively recent financial innovation is the "debit" or "check" card. They look like a credit card but are linked to your checking account. Instead of your purchases accumulating on one monthly bill, they are deducted directly from your checking account. These cards market themselves as offering you the convenience of paying by credit card with the piece of mind offered by paying with a check.

I know these cards are tempting, and I have even used them myself. I must admit, there seems to be more of a sense of control when you deduct your purchases directly from your checking account rather than worrying about one big credit card bill showing up at the end of the month. As tempting as debit cards may be, try to avoid them. There are several good reasons why:

- You will carry piles of receipts in your wallet, purse or pockets that have to be entered into your checkbook.

- Balancing your checking account will become more complicated and time consuming.

- You will inevitably lose or misplace receipts resulting in possible checking account overdrafts.

- If you want to return something, you may not be able to find the receipt, which you separated from the goods to enter in the checkbook.

- They can be costly, as banks may charge a fee for having and using the card.

(The Credit Advantage)

Credit cards can be economical and convenient when selected and used properly. Think about it, you can use someone else's money free of charge, and all you have to do is pay them back on time. You don't need to carry large amounts of cash, and you have the right not to pay when goods or services purchased with your credit card do not meet your expectations. Best of all, you need only write one check each month to pay for everything. With the proper discipline, you may find that adherence to this single principle may be one of the most important steps you take toward simplification.

When you first start this process, you are likely to be taken aback when you open the first bill and see how many purchases you actually make during the month and how much they add up. If you are having a problem with spending, use this to your psychological advantage. Channel the negative emotion about how much money you are spending into positive action.

For example, set a target for yourself to reduce your convenience card bill by say 10% the next month. It's much easier to control something when you know exactly what it is you are trying to control. When all that spending appears on a single piece of paper right in front of your eyes, the message usually hits home.

Principle 5

Value Time, Your Most Important Possession

It seems that a current trend within our society is that we have a little better appreciation for the value of every minute of every day. Many of the things we used to take for granted are just a bit more important to us now, like the time we spend with the ones we love.

While by necessity we must always find time to deal with the realities of everyday life, financial and otherwise, these concerns, although impossible to ignore, should never be our top priority. We may now find ourselves spending less time on these activities so that we have more time to do the things we really enjoy. Simplifying our lives can help us to free up that extra time.

(The Best Laid Plans)

Any self-respecting CPA is going to tell you that you need a good financial plan, right? Wrong! As you will read in the next principle, financial plans done by real financial planners can be a benefit to some people. Unfortunately, many such plans are misguided, far too detailed and complex, and fail to incorporate the goals and objectives that are most important to us.

Personally, I dislike traditional financial plans. They are just too regimented and, like budgets, can be a tremendous source of frustration and disappointment when you fail to meet them.

It is a much more valuable use of time to direct your efforts at first to simplifying your personal financial situation rather than constructing detailed financial plans to deal with the complexity. Once you achieve simplification, you may find that your financial plan is, at a minimum, far less detailed, and quite possibly not needed at all.

(The Top Five)

Does that mean that all financial plans are bad? Certainly not, but before you spend too much time on a financial plan I want you to do the following.

Take a blank piece of paper and write down what the five most important things in your life currently are. I really want you to think about this. Pause for a few minutes and close this book. Only when you are absolutely certain that you have the five most important things written down should you start reading again.

Now look at your list. It's common to see things like family, relationships, job or career, good health, hobbies, school, pets, free time, and even appearance, but money in and of itself generally does not make it. You probably wrote down things that you can't have or do without money, but money itself is most likely not in your top five. Why is it, then, that most of us spend more time planning for and worrying about finances than we spend planning for and worrying about the items on the list?

Does this mean that money is not all that important in the grand scheme of things? Far be it from me to suggest that money is not important. It's very important. The problem is that most of us have developed an obsession with money, and we spend way too much of our time focused on earning, saving, spending, investing, managing and worrying about it. Obsessions with money come in many forms and can range in severity.

(The Compulsive Closet Managers)

We all know people who are obsessed with saving money. This is a disorder with easily recognizable symptoms. It's the compulsive money managers who are much harder to spot.

Many of them mask their disorders well. Hiding out in the privacy of their own homes, alone with their personal finance software programs, they pour over budgets, creating and reviewing detailed financial plans, setting goals, analyzing trends and searching for the perfect investment opportunities. There are an even larger number of otherwise normal, well-adjusted people who, while not obsessed with managing money, have an unhealthy preoccupation with it.

So what's wrong with financial planning and thinking about money? When put in the proper perspective, there's really nothing wrong with it. Most people, however, fail to keep it in the proper perspective. Rather, once they have that detailed financial plan, they consider it to be their road map for life.

A financial plan is far too limiting, as life is about much more than just finances. I always say that I need money to live but I don't live for money. The plan you set for yourself should be a road map from where you are to where you want to be, financial and otherwise. Sure finances will enter into the plan, but they should not consume it.

(Time and Money)

Did you put "time" on your list as one of the things most important to you? Most people would never have thought to include it. That's because time is something we generally don't view as a possession, even though it's one of the most important things we have.

Time is truly our most precious commodity. You can save it or waste it, but once it's gone, it's gone forever. You can spend it on the things you like to do and with the people you love. Unfortunately, aside from our appointment books at work, few of us spend any time planning our time. Rather, we spend most of our time and energy on planning our finances, which doesn't even make the list.

I am not suggesting that money and finances are something that can simply be ignored. If you do that, you may end up spending all your time cleaning up the mess you have made. As you make your way through the pages of this book, however, you will begin to discover that many things that traditional financial thinkers make you believe require a significant amount of time and energy to get "right" may really require a whole lot less of both.

By changing the way you think about certain aspects of managing your money and finances and by making decisions and taking actions that will make things less difficult and complex, you may find that you end up with more of one of the most important possessions you can have — time.

Every day people make decisions between time and money. Some of these decisions are so seemingly insignificant that you might not even realize that they are decisions. For example, maybe you decide to buy a twelve pack of beer at a convenience store for $7.99 when you can get a whole case at the grocery store for $9.99. Perhaps it's your decision to pull in the short-term parking lot at the airport and pay $15 a day rather than walk a few extra steps from the long-term lot that costs $8 a day.

Why do we do these things? Often it's just a matter of convenience. Do these decisions make financial sense? Certainly not, but you make them anyway.

(Clipping Away)

Coupons are another good example of an everyday time versus money decision. I never use coupons. Can using coupons save you money? Sure, you can save a lot of it in fact. We have all seen the stories about someone who buys a couple hundred dollars worth of groceries and gets money back from the store after redeeming all the coupons.

This, however, is surely not the norm. Also, what they don't tell you is that the person would have been financially farther ahead had they invested the same amount of time it took to gather all those coupons working as a cashier at the grocery store.

Rebates are even worse. How many times have you purchased a product because of a rebate offer and failed to collect? In fact, the manufacturers count on it. They make it difficult for you to claim the "rebate prize" by doing things like making you cut out the UPC symbols from the bottom of boxes. Chances are pretty good by the time you get to the bottom you will have forgotten about the rebate or misplaced the redemption form.

Granted, I will never be in a position to potentially save a lot of money with coupons or rebates because I'm unwilling to invest enough time. When it comes to coupons, I have made a time versus money decision, and at this stage in my life, time is simply more important to me.

Being able to recognize and definitively make time versus money decisions is an important step toward simplification. You have to ask yourself, "What's more important in this situation, time or money?" The automatic response is often money but the reasonable response should often be time.

(Time Plans)

Let's talk about time planning for just a moment. What exactly does it mean? Sure you plan meetings at work, doctor appointments, lunch dates and so on. But is this really time planning? I would call this planning your days.

Time planning should encompass a much broader horizon and should incorporate some or all of the items on your list. Remember, that list has on it the five most important things in your life. Say your "family" is one of the things most important to you. Then planning to go on vacation, get out of work in time to attend your child's soccer game, or have your parents over for dinner on Sunday night is considered time planning. Will it take money to make these a reality? In many cases it will, but plan your time first.

Perhaps your job or career made your list. Planning to go to work on Monday morning does not qualify as time planning. Rather, ask yourself some tough questions like "What do I want to be doing 10 years from now and how am I going to get there?" That's time planning.

Maybe your job is important now, but what you really want to do is own your own business. These are the things that most of us never really stop to focus on and consider. Does the thought cross our minds? Sure it does, but it's generally swept away quickly by the realities of daily life, into the abyss of things you should or could have done.

I never used to plan time. Instead I spent all my time planning money. Upon realizing the benefits of simplification, I was finally in a position where I could spend time concentrating on the things that mattered. Eventually I learned how to plan for time. This book is one result.

(New Priorities)

We live in a very complex world. It's easy to get caught up in all of its intricacies. This is especially true in matters of personal finance. I know it's much easier said than accomplished, but you have to work to change your focus, to concentrate less on money and more on the things that made your list of priorities.

You must want to move money out of the forefront and into the background of your life. Strive to put your personal finances safely in control, moving you toward where you want to be, providing for your immediate needs but requiring very little attention or intervention. Only by doing so will you be able to free yourself from the complexity, put aside the detailed financial plans, and focus more on the important things, knowing with confidence that the financial matters are taken care of and secure.

Principle 6

Chose the Best Financial Planner for You

One of the first things people think to do when they come to the conclusion that their personal financial situations are out of control is to enlist the services of a financial planner. Financial plans that are prepared by such planners can vary considerably in size and scope. They can cover long periods of time or short periods. They can deal with all aspects of your personal financial situation or just a few.

In most cases, the end result is a professional-looking package filled with colorful, impressive pie charts and fancy graphs that tell you virtually everything you would ever want to know about your financial situation and a whole lot you probably don't need to know.

(What to Expect)

Financial planners will generally start off by collecting some pretty specific information about your current financial condition. They will need to know everything about you, including how much money you make, what your debts are, what investments you have, how old you are, your family status, as well as details on all your expenses, your pension plan, insurance policies and even the house in which you live.

They will "interview" you to find out how content or discontent you are with your situation. Then they will ask you where you want to be 5, 10, even 30 years from now, focusing primarily on retirement savings, education funding, investing, debt management, insurance and taxes.

Although much of the feedback they provide can be beneficial or at least "eye opening," financial planners generally focus more on telling their clients how to put the pieces of their puzzle together, rather than how to eliminate pieces. In fact, many planners end up suggesting new products or services that can make your puzzle even more complex.

(Population Explosion)

In recent years, there has been an explosion in the popularity of financial planning and, correspondingly, financial planners. It seems that the world is convinced that everyone needs a plan, and there are more than enough people who will put one together.

You can find financial planners at your local bank, insurance agency and broker's office or in comfortable little roadside offices. With the proliferation of inexpensive, sophisticated software, it's easy for anybody to produce financial plans that are very impressive looking just by entering some data and pressing a few buttons. So who are these financial planners anyway?

Basically financial planners can be divided to into three categories:

1. Salespeople

There are many so-called financial planners who are nothing more than salespeople in disguise. They are those people who give you advice on your financial situation while at the same time trying to sell you a product or service that they offer. They work for insurance companies, brokerage houses, mutual funds, banks, and investment managers or operate seemingly as independent "advisors."

Don't be fooled; these "planners" can be well disguised. Seldom will they wear big flashing buttons that say SALESPERSON. Rather, they will work for you with your best interest seemingly at heart, putting together detailed and impressive financial plans for you absolutely free of charge.

Be assured somewhere within that plan will be a recommendation that you need to buy one or more of the products or services that they sell.

If you insist on having a financial plan, try and avoid having a salesperson as a financial planner! It's like asking a farmer who raises chickens what you should have for breakfast. No matter how well intentioned or how honest they may be, the answer will always be "eggs." It's their job to sell you their product, even if it's not what you need.

2. Self-proclaimed

One of the main problems with the financial planning profession is that it really is not a profession at all. Unlike medical doctors, dentists and CPAs, financial planners are not subject to the same extensive state license requirements and regulatory scrutiny. While it is true that salespeople pitching financial products like life insurance and mutual funds must be licensed, they may not be held to the same standards of independence and advocacy for the client as a lawyer or CPA.

Basically anybody can call himself or herself a "financial planner" and basically anybody does. Oftentimes, the competency of self-proclaimed planners can be even more difficult to judge than salespeople disguised as planners. They will usually charge you a fee, either by the hour or a flat rate.

There are plenty of self-proclaimed planners out there, and although they may not be trying to sell you anything, the quality of the services they offer can be dramatically different. Self-proclaimed planners can be anything from people with little or no knowledge of financial matters, to highly trained and experienced advisors with broad-based knowledge of all things financial. Unfortunately, it can be difficult to tell them apart.

3. Professional Planners

There are at least two associations that certify, monitor, and support financial planners and lend needed credibility to the profession. The first is called the Financial Planning Association or FPA, which can be found at www.fpanet.org. The FPA offers a licensing program for members that allows them to use the designation of Certified Financial Planner or CFP.

In order for a planner to use the CFP mark, they must pass a comprehensive certification examination, have several years of experience in the planning profession, voluntarily ascribe to a code of ethics, subject themselves to imposed disciplinary action if they fail to live up to that code, and satisfy certain requirements with regard to continuing education.

The second is the American Institute of Certified Public Accountants or AICPA, which can be found at www.aicpa.org. The AICPA offers a designation of Personal Financial Specialist or PFS. In order to proclaim oneself as a PFS, the planner must be a licensed CPA with an AICPA membership in good standing, meet certain experience requirements working in the capacity of a financial planner, pass a comprehensive examination, submit references, and agree to be bound not only by the ethical standards of the AICPA but also by all standards set forth specific to the PFS designation.

Now let me ask you a question. If you had a toothache would you go to: A) a person who sells dentist drills; B) a person who has a sign hanging outside his office that says "D. Floss. Tooth Repair"; or C) "N.O. Payne, DDS." It seems pretty obvious you would go to Dr. N.O. Payne because you know that those three letters, DDS, mean that Dr. N.O. Payne has achieved a certain level of education, has passed an examination certifying his knowledge, is licensed to practice, and is subject to an ethical code of conduct and disciplinary action.

That does not necessarily mean that Dr. Payne is better than D. Floss or the person who sells dentist drills at being able to fix your tooth. However, that certification or license is oftentimes the only assurance we have.

(Planning Tips)

If you decide that you need a financial plan, just remember to keep the whole process in perspective. It can actually be a good way to inventory all your complexity so that you can begin to sort it all out. Remember what they say about the "best laid plans" however. Therefore, don't become obsessed with achieving the goals or too disappointed if you fail to meet them.

In selecting a planner, keep these guidelines in mind:

- Look for a planner with the CFP or PFS designation.

- If you use a planner without this designation, get several independent recommendations as to the quality of their work.

- Look for a planner who charges a flat fee that is known up front. Watch out for hourly fees or no fees at all.

- If your planner sells products or services or receives bonuses for what you purchase, get a list of what each of those products are. It's nice to know up front why they may be recommending something.

- Never turn assets of any kind over or to the planner or give them access to any personal account information.

(Proper Planning)

Most importantly, inform any planner you are considering up front that you have no interest in simply pushing a bunch of numbers around and ending up with a pretty report that gives you a lot of lofty goals and little direction on how to meet them.

After all, you can accomplish the same thing on your own with an inexpensive planning software package or by accessing the planning models at many financial Web sites. Make sure they understand that you want to make some serious changes in your life and ask them how they intend to help you simplify your financial situation.

Tell them that you are looking to strip away complexity, not manage or add to it, so that you can begin planning for the really important things in life. If they seem unwilling to do anything but put your data into their computer model and generate nice colored charts, say thank you and move on.

Principle 7
Burn the Budget

Virtually every company in the world operates on some type of a budget. Budgets keep businesses under control and focused and provide an excellent tool for measuring progress. They help to identify little problems before they become big problems and can act as an advanced warning system alerting management when things start to go wrong. All that being said, budgets are also a major pain in the butt!

If you operate your household on a formal budget, I want you to think about how much time you spend working on it. Let's see, there is the time you spend putting it all together. Okay, maybe you have a software package to help you. Regardless, you must still go through piles of receipts, canceled checks and bills, make estimates of expenditures, forecast your earnings, plan for major purchases, etc.

Once you have this wonderful budget, then comes the time you must invest in figuring out how well you're performing versus your forecast. Once again, you go through receipts, bank statements, the checkbook, bills, pay stubs and on and on. Then you add it all up and compare actual results to your budget. What inevitably is the result? You are over budget.

It's bad enough that many of us have to deal with budgets from 9 to 5 each day, but it's even more unfortunate when we insist on compounding that pain by bringing a budget into our personal lives. The basic problem with a family budget is that the whole concept just doesn't work very well when applied to living, breathing people.

(Family, Inc.)

Like a corporation, your family has revenues and expenditures, both of which you can attempt to estimate. That's basically where the similarities end. Faced with out-of-control expenses that cause a budget bust, a corporation can make cold and calculated decisions. The sober-faced chairman appears on television agonizing over the human tragedy that will surely result when he pulls the plug on the unprofitable assembly plant that employs more than half the working population of Small Town, USA. Headlines appear the next day, however, in *The Wall Street Journal* proclaiming the virtues of the recently announced, major cost cuts, and the company is often rewarded with an increase in share value.

Faced with stagnant or declining revenues, a corporation can take drastic action to increase its market share by spending millions of dollars on product development or tapping into new markets. Budgets give corporate America goals to strive for and standards by which to judge performance. When things don't go as planned, they take action, serious action in many cases, to put the ship back on course and achieve the results that are expected of them.

If you currently prepare and follow a family budget, think about not only how much time you spend putting it together and analyzing the results but also how much time you and the other members of your family spend talking or thinking about it. I'm not exactly sure why this is, but as a general rule, only one member of a household ever seems passionate about the family budget.

The other members are either moderately interested, couldn't care less about it, or really despise the whole process and wish it would just go away.

(My Budgeting Woes)

If you think that because I'm a CPA my personal finances have always been pretty well buttoned up, guess again. Sure I have tried a couple of times over the years to institute a budget. Every time, however, the result was the same. Not only did I frustrate myself, but I would also drag my unsuspecting wife into the process.

It would begin with my sitting her down at the kitchen table to show her the "numbers." The uncomfortable, pained look on her face was clearly sending me a message, something like "please don't bore me with this" and "you are taking away from my valuable sleep time." Undeterred, I would proceed with the seriousness of a government operative and commence with the interrogation.

"Honey, here are the cold hard facts. This is how much we bring home and this is how much we are spending." I would follow that up with painstakingly detailed, line-by-line analysis of all of our expenditures. The reaction was pretty much the same every time. As her attention faded and eyes began to drift, an occasional yawn would slip. She was clearly uncomfortable with the whole topic and just not that interested.

Not that she is financially irresponsible, just the opposite in fact. However, my analysis and concern over something that she perceived to be, for the most part, out of her control was just something she had no interest in discussing. Her apathy became apparent. "Are you interested in this or not?" I would ask. With a big yawn, the answer was an unconvincing yes.

The interrogation complete, I would deliver the unfortunate verdict. "We are just spending too much money!" The conclusion was clearly not a surprise to her as she had heard it so many times before. Through her big brown eyes I could hear her mind thinking, "All right Joe, just exactly what do you want me to do about it? Maybe we should stop eating or quit putting gas in the car."

The problem is that most people can't stand a budget. They can't spend the time to do it properly, and once they have it, it's already "old news" because things change so rapidly.

At some point I realized that this whole process was getting us absolutely nowhere so I put a stop to it and burned the family budget. All that time I invested in thinking about and preparing my analyses was doing no good. It was a waste of both time and energy, and it was causing family disharmony.

Here I was trying to account for every nickel and dime, only to come to the same conclusion every time. We needed to spend less money. What good was coming from all this? Even when we did try to tighten our belts it didn't seem to make the situation much better because most of the large expenditures that were driving the problems were fixed for an extended period of time. The only things I had immediate control over just didn't have much of an impact.

A word of caution, however: There are many people who allow themselves to get "racheted" up in small, incremental expenses that over the long run add up to a tremendous amount. It can be easy to spend 10, 20, even 50 dollars or more a day on "incidentals" like lunch out, a magazine, a latte, a drink after work, etc. When you spend a little here and a little there, the money dribbles away, and at the end of the month, a lot of presumably unaccounted for money can be lost. We as a generation used to increasing abundance have forgotten how "incremental" spending can suck up a tremendous portion of our incomes. Credit cards make it even easier to spend now and account for it later, sometimes never.

However, will accounting for it change your spending habits? Probably not—the key is to have restraint from the impulse expenses that don't have a good return on expenditure. Try to avoid spending too much on those things that have an immediate gratification but little lasting fulfillment.

(The Human Factor)

Everyone has days, weeks, months and even years where unexpected expenditures can get the best of you. Those things will happen and, unless you are being frivolous or irresponsible, you may just have to accept it.

Say the tires are wearing on your car and your daughter loses a filling in her tooth. If you were a corporation you might decide that "the tires will last another 10,000 miles so let's not change them right away" and "your daughter can chew on the other side of her mouth for a while." Both are cold and calculated economic decisions based not upon human emotion but concern for the bottom line. The problem is that your spouse drives that car to get to work every day on the expressway and it needs to be safe, and your daughter is in terrible discomfort.

So what do you do? You get new tires and fill the tooth of course, even if you really don't have the extra money. It's an emotional decision. Agonizing over this unbudgeted expense and sharing that agony with everyone else in the family is surely not the right answer.

Sometimes these emotional decisions are made based not upon need but more upon what makes you feel good. Say your child wants a new pair of sneakers so you go to the mall and he or she picks out a pair of $80 Nike shoes. What do you do?

If you were a corporation, perhaps you would perform a cost/benefit analysis to determine whether or not $80 is too much to pay for a pair of sneakers. You might also put out for competitive bids, selecting the most economical pair that meets your minimum requirements for comfort and functionality.

The problem is that you are not a corporation but a live person with emotions that play a part in just about every decision you make, financial or otherwise. One of the largest industries in America, the marketing and advertising business, is targeting directly at your emotions. Their sales pitch is directly aimed at the subliminal "impulse" buy.

When you are faced with a dilemma caused by their marketing manipulation, it may be hard to resist. Sure your child will survive in the lower priced sneakers, but the look on his or her face when you say that it is okay to get the Nikes may be worth the difference in cost at that instant. Many highly paid advertising psychologists are betting on this fact. The problem is not just in that one purchase; it is in the aggregation of many of those purchases.

The bottom line is that, unlike a corporation, almost every decision we make about our personal finances is impacted by emotion. These decisions are not predicated purely upon analysis of the bottom line but more upon what makes you happy and satisfied. This is one of the reasons family budgeting is so difficult.

(The Kid, The Car, The Condo)

A formal budget requires a significant investment of time. Much of this time amounts to nothing more than counting up the "nickels and dimes" of everyday living. People devote hours each month to figuring out how much they spend on common expenditures like lunches, gasoline, utility bills, and dry cleaning. For an occasional exercise using the simple technique discussed in principle 4, it is probably a good idea.

However, for a monthly exercise, it is a needless torture. In the grand scheme of things, most of these expenditures are fixed and thus out of people's immediate control.

Evaluating where your money is going is a good idea if done periodically. Evaluating how you spend the "disposable" income makes sense, as long as you don't take it to the extreme.

Can you save a few dollars a month by threatening every member of your household with bodily harm should they leave a light on in an empty room, turn the thermostat above 65, or stay in the shower for more than 10 minutes? Sure you can, but before you go down this path ask yourself if the result is really worth the time you will invest and aggravation you will inflict upon yourself and other members of your family who must live under your police state.

Look at the "disposable" or discretionary money that you spend and use that as a pool of savings. Rather than chasing the electric bill by turning off all the lights, look at the premium cable package and ask yourself if the benefit is worth the cost.

For example, consider the latte habit. It could cost $1,000 per year if you buy one latte each day. Is it worth it? Is the premium cable at $70 per month ($840 per year) really worth it? If you didn't have it, would your lifestyle change that much? Add up all these incremental savings as a learning exercise, and you will be surprised at the results.

Once you have dealt with the "discretionary" expenses, you can begin to focus on the broader issues that really impact your personal finances. It's the **big** financial events that occur and decisions that we make that have real impact.

As you will read in the principles that follow, I believe there are three major events and decisions that basically determine our financial condition and are responsible for the majority of financial problems. I refer to them as "spending blockbusters." They are:

- Whether or not you have children

- The kind of car you drive

- The house in which you live

If people understand the impact of these blockbusters and learn how to make reasonable and informed decisions to minimize the negative financial consequences of these three important things, most will have no need to perform the endless and time-consuming analysis of events that are less significant and often uncontrollable. There will be more on the spending blockbusters in the principles that follow. Once you learn to control them, you will find the need for a formal budget will be significantly diminished or even eliminated.

(Easy Budget)

Since it is a good idea to know the general nature of what is draining the bank account each month, I suggest doing a simple analysis every so often. All you need is a piece of paper and a pen. Throw away old receipts, bills, pay stubs, tax returns and turn off your computer, as you won't need them.

At the top of that piece of paper, simply write down your monthly take-home income. Now list all of your monthly recurring expenses including all the "big things" like mortgage, property or additional income taxes you will owe, car payments, insurance, electric, cable, phone, food, gasoline, day care. Then all the "little things" like dry cleaning, Internet access fees, health

73

club memberships, parking, commuting, babysitters, magazine subscriptions, lunch, etc.

Use the technique discussed in principle 4. You should easily be able to find all these recurring expenditures just by using your "convenience card" account statement and checkbook.

Now subtract your total monthly expenditures from your take-home income. What is left over we will refer to as your monthly "cushion." This isn't exactly brain surgery here, folks! What you have done is calculate the money that should be available each month to pay for unexpected (tires for the car, furnace repair), emotional (the $80 Nikes, concert tickets), and seasonal (holiday time, back-to-school shopping) spending.

Take the amount of your cushion, write it on a piece of paper and stick it up on the side of your refrigerator. Now, every time you have an unexpected, emotional or seasonal spending event occur, subtract that amount from your total cushion. You only need to keep track of the cushion. When it's gone, it's gone.

You should expect that some months your cushion might disappear long before you turn the page of the calendar. As long as you are spending responsibly, just accept the fact that you may have to dip into savings or rely upon your credit card. Try not to dwell on or worry about the cushion being gone. Accept what has happened, figure out how to balance out the month and move on.

This is really all the budget analysis most people need to run their household. In fact, it's still more analysis than most people need unless you are planning to incorporate your family. The point is, we get too caught up in analyzing the numbers. The numbers will take care of themselves for the most part once you learn how to control the spending blockbusters and the emotional "impulse" buys.

Principle 8
Control Emotional Spending

So you reached that crisis point in your life where you have finally concluded beyond all doubt that you must be doing something wrong. You have worked all those years only to find yourself still in the same basic financial situation you were in years earlier. Sure you have a nice house, new car, furniture in every room and even a few dollars tucked away, but you are still a long way from where you want to be and time is running out.

Every Monday you drag yourself out of bed and head off to a job that doesn't pay or satisfy you enough. It seems that you worry about money constantly and have nightmares about having to work as the greeter at Wal-Mart after you retire just so you can afford to buy groceries.

As if things weren't bad enough, one of those aggravating articles appears in the Money pages of your local newspaper to reinforce your discontentment. You know the type. Generally they go something like the following.

(The Financially Perfect Family)

Meet John and Debbie, both 40. John works as a technician for an imaging company and Debbie is an administrative assistant at a law firm. Their combined income is $75,000. They have one child and live in a modest home in the suburbs. John has $45,000 in his 401(k), and Debbie has another $20,000. They hold mutual funds valued at $35,000, an impressive stock portfolio, $20,000 tucked away in Series EE bonds to pay for college education, and $10,000 in several IRAs. Both work for companies with pension plans. "So how much more money do they need to save to retire at age 60?" the article asks.

"Who are these people," you ask yourself, "and do they write articles about them for any other reason than to depress me?" These must be financial freaks of nature that have invaded from some distant planet.

After all, you and your spouse make about the same amount as John and Debbie and likewise live in a modest house. That, unfortunately, is where the similarities end. For unlike John and Debbie, you have virtually nothing put away for college or for retirement with the exception of the modest balance in your 401(k). You still live paycheck to paycheck most weeks, struggling at times just to pay the bills without dipping into your savings. You have a couple of mutual funds and a modest, under-performing stock portfolio.

You try not to think about having to pay for college because it makes you physically ill to do so. Thoughts of retirement cause you to break out in a rash. You have credit card bills, a furnace that needs to be replaced, a home equity loan that needs to be repaid, and lease payments on the minivan to make.

Buying ground beef or ground round is still a major financial decision to you. Your fate has somehow been sealed, and this article just confirms it. You are so far behind the curve it is futile to even try to catch up; all you can do is hope that Social Security doesn't go bankrupt. So what have you done wrong?

(Natural Instincts)

When it comes to money, I find there are generally two types of people in this world. There are those who like to save it and those who like to spend it. I do not belittle people who can save money. In fact, quite the opposite, I respect those who manage to put something away for the future. On a personal level, however, I tend to dislike savers, intimidated by their habits.

You see, I'm about as far removed from being a saver as could be. I do manage to put some money away on occasion, but for me it's an extremely difficult proposition. Every time I put money aside I view it is as taking away from something I could be doing that's inevitably more fun. I'm the type of guy who can't walk through Home Depot without wanting to buy a new lawn mower, even though there may be absolutely nothing wrong with the one I have. I start looking for my next car on the way home from picking up my new one.

I get a charge out of buying stuff. It lifts my spirits and makes me feel good. Although I am financially responsible, I see money as something that is to be spent on the things that make me happy and on the people who are most important to me.

Most of us have absolutely no problem spending money. In fact, we generally find spending money to be a whole lot more fun than saving. Herein lies the fundamental problem. The emotional gratification people get from buying far exceeds the satisfaction of saving. We are seemingly predisposed to spending money.

Unless you are truly a compulsive saver, it's probably been a long time since you got excited about opening up your bank statement. Now think about buying a high-definition television, new furniture or how about a new car? That's a whole other matter all together. For the vast majority of us, it's a constant battle between the power of financial reason and the satisfaction of a good purchase.

Spenders tend to make critical mistakes, especially when it comes to dealing with the "spending blockbusters" and can manage to get themselves in trouble when confronted with less significant purchases.

(Keeping Your Cool)

You stumble to the refrigerator one morning, open the door and take out the milk to pour in your coffee. Something is terribly wrong, as the milk carton feels warm. "It's a twenty-year-old appliance," the repairman tells you. "It's just not worth fixing." Off to the appliance store you go.

The salesperson shows you a perfectly adequate 20 cubic foot model for $530 that is virtually identical to the one that broke. Looks pretty good, but you really would like one with glass shelves and an icemaker. No problem, for $780 you can get it. Oh look, there's a side-by-side with a water dispenser and icemaker built right in the door. Wouldn't that be convenient? You can get it in white-on-white complete with a night light for only $955.

While you're at it, you decide to look at microwaves. The old one is starting to show its age and will look pretty bad next to that brand new refrigerator. Come to think about it, the dishwasher is ready to go, too. As long as you have to pull out the dishwasher, why not replace the countertops? A hard-core spender can easily turn a $530 refrigerator into a $10,000 kitchen, complete with new floors, cabinetry, lighting fixtures and even coordinating dishtowels.

How does this happen? Spenders get caught up in the emotion of the purchase decision and lose their sense of financial reason. The refrigerator was simply the first step that pushed the ball into motion. A whole new kitchen is the end result.

(An Unnatural Act)

Chances are pretty good that at some point along the way you have made a commitment to yourself to start saving more money. Resigning yourself to a pattern of self-inflicted savings is not all bad. It's good to have "saving money" as a goal provided that you identify a means by which to achieve it.

The problem for most of us, however, is not necessarily saving money but spending money. Anyone can spend money but few people do it responsibly or correctly. Most people tend to follow the "chameleon principle." They quickly adapt their habits and lifestyle to their income level. It seems to be a natural instinct. One of the truest adages ever spoken is: "The more money you make the more you must spend."

Face it—the odds of saving money are stacked against you. It's just not that easy to do. With all this going against us we must find a way to overcome it. Spending money is a natural reaction triggered by our search for satisfaction. Like other instant reactions, at times it must be suppressed and controlled.

I'm not about to give you a bunch of suggestions for cutting back your spending. There are plenty of traditional books about personal finance that will offer you all kinds of advice on that. The important message here is to learn to respect and control the emotional power spending money can have over you. Concentrate your efforts on those spending decisions that have the biggest impact, the "spending blockbusters," and learn to master the emotions that impact those decisions.

(Emotional Line of Credit)

If you find yourself having trouble controlling spending, there's a little trick you can play on yourself that just may work. It's an unfortunate reality that most people use credit cards not just for convenience but also as a source of borrowing. No matter how well you manage debts, there's always a sense of uneasiness that accompanies carrying a balance. That's exactly why most responsible people find themselves desperately trying to pay off their outstanding balance in full each month.

So at the risk of contradicting one of the most basic and fundamental principles of personal finance, getting rid of credit card debt, I suggest to you that this may not always be the best thing to do. You can actually use the guilt associated with carrying a balance to your advantage.

Paying off your balance in full each month frees up your "emotional line of credit." When you don't already owe, you are much more likely to go out and spend more. It's like having a pocketful of cash. When you have an outstanding balance, guilt takes over and you must stop to think before you pull that card out of your wallet.

So if you are having a problem with spending or seem continually unable to find any extra money to put away, you may just want to consider carrying a balance on your low-interest financing card. Play the negative emotion and guilt of carrying your balance to your full advantage.

If you are going to give this a try, make sure you follow the advice in principle 4 and select one and only one financing card.

Do not consider any card that has an annual fee or a high rate of interest.

(Spending Diet)

When it comes to spending and savings, here are the most important things to remember:

- You will never learn to save unless you first learn how to spend.

- The emotional gratification of spending far exceeds that of saving.

- A small number of critical spending decisions are generally responsible for the majority of financial problems.

To say that you will simply stop or limit spending after years of abuse is as likely to fail as saying you are going to start a diet after years of uncontrolled eating. The natural forces working against you are too strong. There is more to it than that.

Just like the dieter who goes from chicken wings and fries on Monday to an ounce of turkey and carrot sticks on Tuesday, failure is imminent in most cases. There is no cold turkey option when it comes to spending money. It is impossible to walk away from it completely. You must attain a level of satisfaction with your spending habits that you can live with or you will always find yourself wanting more.

As you proceed through these principles and start making changes that will lead you down the road toward personal financial simplicity, always remember and respect the importance of spending. For if you are able to successfully control the emotion of spending, you will have set down the cornerstone upon which to begin your journey back to simplicity.

Principle 9
Keep Your Money Out of Sight

So you are 30 pounds overweight and you decide you're going to do something about it. You go on one of those diets where you eat a handful of carrots for breakfast, a handful of celery sticks for lunch and a "sensible" four-ounce broiled chicken breast for dinner.

As a special treat, you get a serving of broccoli with some fake spray butter on top. Then you plunk down $300 to join the local health club, where you start going every other morning before work for a 45-minute sprint on the treadmill.

Will you lose 30 pounds? It's entirely possible. Will you keep the weight off and stick to the diet and exercise regime? It's highly unlikely. A common mistake people make when trying to lose weight is that they go to extremes and end up doing something that is radically different from what they have been used to doing. Only a rare individual with exceptional will power can keep it up over the long term.

Just like dieting, saving money is inherently difficult. In the last principle, I described how you must do battle with extremely powerful emotional forces working against you if you are to be successful at saving money. Just like going from burgers and fries one day to carrots and celery the next is destined to fail, going from uncontrolled spending one day to trying to save everything the next is equally doomed. You must accept how difficult saving money is likely to be and look for ways to make the process as painless as possible.

The first step in trying to save money is to figure out just exactly how much you have to save. Back in principle 7, I asked you to calculate your monthly spending "cushion," which is your leftover money available to pay for unplanned expenditures and emotional purchases. It's also your source for potential savings. Unless you happen to be a compulsive saver, you are going to have to fight off the natural predispostion toward wanting to spend that cushion, and instead try to put it away.

So you want to save money but it "just seems to burn a hole in your pocket" or perhaps you just never know "where it all goes." Is there anything you can do? I believe there are two keys to painless savings. The first is to limit accessibility. It is much more difficult to become emotionally attached to something you have never seen or touched. Limit your access to your "cushion" of emotional money, and you will significantly reduce the pain associated with not being able to spend it.

(Save with Uncle Sam)

How do you do it? Get ready, because here's one that will make virtually every traditional financial advisor shake their head in bewilderment and wonder how I ever passed the CPA exam. My recommendation is really quite simple. Have more tax money withheld from your pay than is necessary. That's right; let the government hold your money.

Why would you ever let the federal government hold on to your money? Seems every January you hear the experts advising us that now is the time to change your withholdings if you are expecting a refund. Why give the government an interest-free loan, they ask? You can keep that money in your own pocket, invest it, or pay off your debt.

I don't dispute for an instant the economic viability of this advice. Once again, however, personal finance is not just about pure economics; it's about emotion. Therefore, if you are having a problem saving money, I say ignore the experts and let the government hold your money. It's a simple way to save.

Just take some percentage of your "cushion" that you are reasonably confident will not have to be spent and let Uncle Sam keep it for you until tax time. Just go down to your payroll department and tell them exactly how much more you want withheld and have your withholding adjusted accordingly.

Go ahead and set yourself up for a nice big tax refund. The real challenge is then going to be what you do with the money once it arrives. If you spend it on a trip to Las Vegas, then perhaps you have accomplished nothing. Here again, however, is where emotion plays such a big part in the spending and saving process, and why this strategy may just work for you when other attempts at saving money have failed.

Say you decide to have $50 extra withheld each week and end up getting back a refund check for $2,600, a decent sum of money by any measure. You might decide to use it all to pay off a credit card. Emotionally, that's a very satisfying use of that money and chances are it will make you feel pretty good about yourself.

Alternatively, you can follow traditional advice and keep that $50 in your pocket each week. Ask yourself honestly, what do you think the chances are that the extra $50 would have been used to pay down a credit card bill? Although your answer may be yes, chances are pretty good that the reality will be no.

There is very little emotional satisfaction in applying $50 each week to your credit card. The satisfaction from a $50 night out to dinner and a movie would be much greater. The same goes for investing that $50 each week in a mutual fund. That too does little to get the satisfaction index rising. Putting $2,600 in all at once or buying 100 shares of a favorite stock may be a whole different matter. That can rank potentially high on the satisfaction index.

Sometimes it is necessary to take some seemingly irrational action like letting the IRS hold your money just to counter the emotional and practical realities with which you are dealing.

(Keep Your Distance)

There are certainly other ways you can emotionally detach yourself from your money. For example, set up automatic payments to savings accounts, mutual funds and dividend reinvestment funds. Although not bad ideas, the basic problem with these options is that access to the money is not really restricted. If you just can't bring yourself to let the government save your money or if you have the discipline to keep your hands out of the cookie jar, then these are viable options.

You can also put money away in IRAs, 401(k)s, stock purchase plans, savings bond purchase programs, and other places. Many of these plans, especially those that are employer sponsored, can have lucrative benefits associated with them, and you should participate.

You must also work to reduce the opportunities that you give yourself to spend money. This may sound all too obvious, but a major reason why people fail to save money is that they simply give themselves far too many chances to spend it!

Take those trips to the mall for instance. Inevitably, you will see things that you "need" to buy. Things you really didn't need until you saw them. Once the emotion takes over and you have convinced yourself that you need or want something, it's very difficult to resist buying it.

For many, it seems that our natural inclination when we are bored or depressed is to shop. Consider a Saturday afternoon bike ride through the park as an alternative. If the weather's bad, go to a movie. It will probably cost you a lot less.

(An Interest in Savings)

You can also look for ways to make saving money emotionally satisfying. That is, make your savings more like purchasing. If you are a NASCAR fan, consider buying stock in a company like International Speedway Corporation (ISCA), which operates several major tracks. If you are thinking of a new set of titanium irons, maybe buy a few shares of Callaway Golf (ELY) instead. You may even be one of those fortunate people who can find an interest that actually lets you invest and spend money at the same time, for example, if you enjoy restoring old cars or collecting art.

I am not suggesting that you go out and buy shares of companies just because they are in an industry that you happen to like or that you show up at the local auction house and bid on expensive pieces of art about which you know nothing. If these investments perpetually lose money, any satisfaction you may have derived from buying them will quickly fade away. What I am suggesting is that if you have a difficult time saving money, you must search for ways to do it that are as emotionally satisfying and rewarding as spending.

Let's face it; for most of us, putting cash away in a money market fund each month, although noble, is far from exciting. You may need to spice up your savings habits. Save by investing in things that are interesting to you.

The psychology and emotion behind our attitudes toward money are powerful things. Unless you fully understand what you are up against and prepare yourself to deal with it, it will be difficult to change your spending habits and achieve your savings objectives. Do not overcomplicate the task. Although you will be unable to completely suppress the forces of human emotion that feed your desire to buy and spend, with a few simple steps, you will manage to master and control it.

This leads us to the second key. Once you learn to limit the opportunities you give yourself to spend, you must find ways to make your spending (and savings) experiences more rewarding. For example, force yourself to put off buying that new car until the old one is paid off completely. Suffer through one more year with your 20-inch television and broken remote until you have enough money saved to go out and pay cash to buy a new one. Search for low-cost items that can bring hours of enjoyment, like books and CDs. If you are really frugal, use the public library. They generally have great collections of books, some even have CDs and movies, and it is essentially free.

You get the idea. Find ways to make your buying experiences satisfying and explore ways to satisfy yourself that do not require buying. You will never hear me advocate a complete ban on emotional spending. If you can do it, great, but it's not for me. I need the emotional lift spending brings every once in a while. Rather, make limited and intelligent spending decisions that are high on satisfaction and low on financial stress.

Principle 10
Don't Become House Poor

The reason most of us manage to get ourselves into financial difficulty and end up complicating our lives is that we just plain spend too much money. Although spending abuse can take many forms, the average family can trace most of their problems back to one or more of several major events. These are events in your life that cause you to open your wallet and keep it that way for years in the future. The first of these "spending blockbusters" is the place you call home.

(Over Time Means Overnight)

Perhaps you bought your first house with a plan to remodel it over time. Unfortunately, the reality can be far different from the plan, and the financial effects can be long lasting and devastating. The old carpets in the living room weren't exactly to your taste so you figured to replace them "someday." The hardwood floors in the dining room would really look beautiful refinished. New cabinets, countertops and appliances would make all the difference in the kitchen, and the harvest-gold sinks and toilets and bathrooms really need to go as well. Again, this could all be done "over time."

For some unknown reason the concepts of "someday" and "over time" somehow become overnight, and before you know it, your house is undergoing a complete transformation right before your eyes. From window treatments to wall coverings, it all begins to change, and once it starts, momentum builds. Worse yet, it usually happens during that period of time when you are still learning to adjust to your new mortgage payment and can least afford these large expenditures.

Since your house is generally the single largest purchase you will ever make, it seems perfectly logical that it can also be the single largest financial mistake you will ever make. Many,

many people do just that. They make a big mistake when choosing a home and greatly underestimate the amount of money that will be spent paying for fixing, remodeling and keeping it up.

We all want to have a nice, comfortable place to live in to raise our families and call home. There is probably no purchase easier to emotionally attach to than a house, and the all-important financial considerations are oftentimes overlooked.

Don't look for the mortgage company to rescue you either. Remember that when it comes to financing your home purchase, lenders will give you just about as much rope as you want. A $2,000 limit increase on your credit card may take an act of Congress, but ask for a $200,000 mortgage and they will knock each other over to get your business.

(Too Much House Can Mean Too Little Money)

So what do many people do? They take most of the rope and end up buying a house that is both more than they need and more than they can afford. Now, having a nice house is wonderful but having a big mortgage payment is not.

As hard as it is going to be, you must try and interject a little reason into this extremely important financial decision. Ask yourself, "If I'm paying a $1,800 a month mortgage payment just how much money will be left over to do the things I want to do?" Perhaps you like to go out to dinner, take nice vacations and drive new cars. Before you ever sign those papers picture yourself sitting at the kitchen table some Friday night with checkbook in hand and calculator on the table. You have just figured out that you simply won't have any extra money for a very long time.

Do you know how depressing it can get when you go to work every day just to pay the mortgage? As emotionally satisfying as buying a new house can be, it can be even more emotionally demoralizing when you realize that you can no longer afford to buy anything else.

So what should you do? Simply be reasonable at purchase time by divorcing yourself from the emotion of the decision and projecting into the financial reality of the future. Overestimate what the house is going to cost you. If you are at or near the limit of what the lender is willing to give you, chances are pretty good that you are buying too much house.

(Running out of Room)

The biggest problem most people have with a house and the reason they start looking for a new one is that they run out of room—not room for the people but room for their stuff. So what do they do? They buy a bigger house of course. However, what most people need is not a bigger house but simply more places to put the stuff. A smaller, organized, uncluttered house can be a significantly more tranquil, satisfying and financially viable place to be.

This may sound ridiculous, but trust me on this one. When looking at the features of a house, one of your top priorities should be the amount of useable storage space. I don't care if you're just starting out or ready to retire, there is no house you can buy with too much storage space. Go all the way back to principle 2. Having things well organized is one of the keys to simplification. Things will be easier to deal with if they are neat and in order.

This applies as much to your financial documents as it does to your closet. While you're at it, don't forget to apply the rest of principle 2. Go through those closets every so often and get rid of what you don't use any more.

Storage space doesn't just mean walk-in closets and an attic. With a little imagination you can easily create orderly storage space just about anywhere.

You may be able to access unused space above your garage by installing a pull down stairway, construct storage closets in your basement for seasonal clothes and permanent shelving to safely store holiday decorations, luggage, tools and boxes. Extra linen closets often can be built into empty space between existing walls.

You can also do amazing things in your closets with those wire rack organizers. Put hooks just about anywhere and get everything from bicycles and snow shovels to garden tools and patio chairs off the ground where they take up valuable floor space.

So when you are out looking for a new house, make sure that you add to the top of your list of most important features the number of square feet of useable storage space. Tell the Realtor that you must have the total square footage and a detailed listing of all suitable storage including dry basement areas, an easily accessible attic, clean and usable crawl spaces, clothes and linen closets, pantries, permanent sheds, etc.

Calculate a percentage and use this as a point of comparison to other houses at which you are looking. After all, one big closet may be all that separates you from having to write out one big mortgage payment every month.

(The Pay Off)

While I'm on the topic of housing costs, let's address the subject of prepaying your mortgage. As a general rule, I don't look favorably upon prepaying a mortgage. Remember our annoying couple John and Debbie? They aspire to be debt free by the time they reach 50. As such, virtually every spare penny they have goes to pay down their mortgage debt. Well good for them!

It's an admirable goal to be mortgage free and psychologically satisfying to own your home free and clear. For most people, however, it's simply not realistic to think they can prepay their mortgage appreciably faster without diverting funds from repaying other higher priced sources of borrowing or putting some cash away for a rainy day. For them, prepaying their mortgage debt should not be a priority.

With its competitive rate and tax deductibility, mortgage debt is generally the cheapest form of borrowing you will ever have. So unless it's realistic to think you can pay it off, relax. For more information on mortgage shopping and rates, visit Web sites like www.lendingtree.com and www.e-loan.com.

Even if you can afford to do it, this may not be a good idea. Of course, absent the crystal ball that allows you to project the returns on alternative places to put your money, it's only possible to say for sure with the benefit of hindsight. All debts are not created equal, and as far as mortgages go, they aren't such a bad form of debt.

(The Beauty of New)

New home construction can be a viable, attractive option for many potential homebuyers. Make no mistake, however: Building a new home is time consuming and emotionally and financially draining. If you are seriously considering it, knowing what to expect up front will make it a less stressful experience for everyone involved.

For some, building new is the only option. From the floor plan to the wall colors, you can have everything just the way you want it. No need to worry about leaking hot water tanks, furnaces that won't stay lit, windows that won't seal, and roofs that need repair. Everything will be brand new, spotlessly clean and in perfect working order the day you move in. At least you hope it will be.

Let me give you a few lessons I learned in the school of new home construction. Keep these keys to a successful home building experience in mind right from the start, and you should be able to avoid or at least prepare yourself for the pitfalls, minefields and booby traps that lie ahead.

Select the Right Builder.

Whether you want to or not, you are going to have to develop a working relationship with your builder. New home construction is a cooperative effort and the fact is that some builders are just more cooperative than others.

Before you sign on the dotted line, meet with your builder several times, preferably in his or her office where you get an opportunity to see how customers, suppliers, and employees are dealt with first hand. If you don't connect on a personal level, then look for someone else. Get references and follow up on them. Watch the classified ads in your local business newspaper to see if there is a "mechanic's lien" filed against a builder. Call the local building inspector to ask if there have been any problems with the builder that you are considering.

For our second home, we choose a local builder with an excellent reputation and proven track record, as opposed to one of the large national chain builders. At David Homes, the owner of the company was directly involved in all phases of the construction process, which works to your advantage especially if you are looking to customize your home. There can be risks when dealing with smaller builders if they do not have a demonstrated history of past success. Do your homework.

Master the art of compromise and the virtue of patience.

You will need to learn how to compromise. It's inevitable; there will be things you want in your new home that for some reason you will just not be able to have.

You will also have to make plenty of decisions. It's almost unimaginable how many things you have to pick out during a very short period of time. Many of them relate to features that you never paid much attention to, like the color of siding, the shingles on the roof, facade, sinks, countertops, doorhandles, moldings, windows, even the doorbell.

You will also need a good dose of patience. Make sure you have it, not only with your builder but also with subcontractors, the suppliers and most importantly with your spouse. It's virtually inevitable that someone will make a mistake or take more time than agreed on to get something done.

Get it in Writing

For our first home, we choose a builder without doing much investigation into his reputation, and we paid the price. I remember one day we arrived at the construction site to find that windows and screens had been delivered. I was concerned since they were clearly visible from the street and sitting in an unlocked garage. Sure enough the next day we returned and the screens were gone. Someone had apparently stolen them! Little did I know that it was our builder who had done it. They had been returned to the window distributor for credit. I was informed that the screens were not included in our contract.

Well, is the glass included in the windows? Make sure you get *everything* in writing, even things that you may think are obvious.

The process of constructing a new home is extremely complex. No matter how hard you try to keep things in control, inevitably things will slip through the cracks. Through all phases of planning your new home, take detailed notes of all discussions with the builder, especially when it comes to features or options that he says are included. Some builders are notorious for trying to cut corners wherever and whenever possible. Not that all builders are like this, but you probably won't know what yours is like for sure until it's too late.

Make sure ceiling heights and room, hallway, closet, foyer, door, and window dimensions are clearly marked on the blueprints. Get a list of specific construction materials in the contract, including composition of the foundation; type of lumber used for studs, flooring, and walls; methods of construction (nailed, screwed, glued); and roofing materials to name a few. Have someone who understands it, like a home inspector, look it over for you.

Allowances for lighting, flooring, cabinetry and plumbing fixtures should be spelled out specifically. Restrictions, if any, on where you can spend those allowances should also be specified.

Make a list of all the less obvious items that you may not automatically think of that should be spelled out in the contract. Basically every detail should be clearly specified in the blueprints, the contract or attached to the contract in a separate document that both you and the builder have signed. Take nothing for granted.

Expect to Pay More

Expect that everything is going to cost you more than you thought it would. Remember your first trip through the builder's model home? Everything looked so beautiful. Just remember, models generally include all the extras.

Builders are not about to let you walk through a stripped down model, as they want you to see and experience the best. As you walk through a builder's model remember that just about everything you are looking at is an upgrade.

Know Your Allowances

You will quickly discover one thing about your allowances. They are simply not enough. In case you don't know, this is a generic term used to describe the amount of money that the builder gives you to spend on things like flooring, carpeting and lighting. Worse yet, most builders cut deals with suppliers like lighting stores. That means your allowance can only be spent at higher priced "specialty stores" rather than at Home Depot. Before you settle on a builder, do your homework on the allowances. Find out how much they are and where you have to spend them, then figure how far they will go based upon the prices for the quality you want.

All allowances are not created equal, and they can be an important factor in determining the true cost of your new home. Remember, too, if you run over on allowances, you must pay cash or charge them. Big allowances built into the contract can become part of the mortgage, so if cash is an issue, ask your builder to increase the allowances and add it to the selling price.

Build at the Right Time of Year

Most people think about building a new home in the springtime, when all of our thoughts turn to things that are new. If you want complexity in your life, try doing things at the same time that everybody else is. The same goes for building a house. There are many good reasons for starting construction of your new home during the springtime. Unfortunately, the new home construction market is filled with anxious customers.

As the season heats up, the demands on the time of the builder, his contractors and suppliers will become even more severe. There will be inevitable delays, rescheduling and missed appointments. Your builder is likely to forget a thing or two along the way. Subcontractors will rush to get to the job and rush to get done with it. The results? Quality is likely to be low and your frustration level with the builder will be high.

So what's the answer? Build when everyone else is still just thinking about it. This will depend on where you live. You should have your builder's undivided attention, and the chances of getting things right will be much improved.

Get Things Done Before You Move In

Once the builder has your money, it will be much more difficult to get him to devote attention to your problems. Make sure all work is completed to your satisfaction before you close the sale. If you can't wait to close, make sure any remaining work is detailed in writing and incorporated in the closing documents. The best contracts have penalty clauses that can be invoked should the builder fail to complete things on time.

Add language to say if the work is not complete by the date indicated you have the right to have someone else of your choice complete it and bill it to the builder. You should consider a hold-back of some of the proceeds until the work is complete. That is, hold some of the cash purchase price back that can be used to pay contractors you may have to hire to complete work that does not get done on time.

(To Build or Not to Build)

So have I managed to discourage you sufficiently enough so that building a new home is no longer an option? Probably not, if you were already considering building a new home, chances are that even the worst horror stories will do little to deter you.

Building a new home can be a rewarding experience provided you have the time and energy to devote to the process. Make sure you choose a builder with whom you can work and do your homework before you commit.

(Model Solution)

Is there a better option for people looking for a home that will immediately satisfy their needs, comes with few surprises and has none of the hassles associated with older homes? You bet there is, and it's called the model home. Builders use model homes to showcase floor plans, styles and quality of construction. They also tend to fill these homes with all the finishing touches for which you would pay thousands of dollars extra if you built with them from scratch.

Buying a model is a good idea if you want a new home but don't want to deal with the complexity that goes with building it. You will also know what you are getting up front and often you will get a whole lot more. Hire a home inspector to go through and you will immediately find out the quality of construction materials, workmanship, the structural integrity, and if all the mechanical elements are properly installed. Builders can also be far more flexible when it comes to model homes, not only on price but also on terms and conditions of sale, making the whole experience less stressful.

(Choose Wisely)

Regardless of what you decide to do, never underestimate the potentially devastating effect that a house can have on your personal financial situation. Whether you opt for very old, brand new, or something in between, be prepared to spend money for years to come.

Do not overestimate what kind of house you "need" or get too caught up in the emotions of what you want. Oftentimes, a bigger, more expensive house may seem like the solution, but in reality it ends up just adding to the problem.

Principle 11

Keep in Mind the Costs of Raising a Family

Not only is parenting an incredible emotional journey, it's also a pretty remarkable financial journey as well. You have never really learned how to spend money until you have a child. It begins innocently enough but soon escalates to an all-out assault on your finances and certainly qualifies as another "spending blockbuster."

(The Economics of Parenting)

When a child is very little, the impact may be barely noticeable. If you are fortunate enough to be the beneficiary of a baby shower, or if your have a brother, sister or friends who have recently completed their early parenting years, much of what you need for the first year may be given or loaned to you. If you do have to go out and buy things like a crib, playpen, stroller or car seat, be prepared. Chances are that you will want the best and safest of everything, and none of it comes cheap.

Diapers, wipes and formula will cost you plenty, too. For the first few months, especially if you are breast-feeding, the impact on your finances should be manageable, as the adjustment to your lifestyle is far more significant than the adjustment to your pocketbook. As time goes on, however, the impact begins to grow.

From toys and games to coats and shoes, the floodgates start to open around age two and stay open for many years to come. There will be dance, gymnastics, and karate lessons to take, musical instruments to play, sports equipment to buy, and presents to give. Your definition of vacation will change from a week sitting on the beach to going someplace with rides, preferably lots of rides, and fireworks—someplace that charges you $40 a day or more just to get in and $4 for Coke once you do.

As children journey through the teenage years, the costs and expenses begin to escalate. Once they gain a sense of fashion, get ready for the $80 sneakers, $60 jeans and $30 cotton t-shirts. You may be asked to finance trips to the hair stylist, weekend getaways with friends, skateboards, roller blades, mountain bikes, class trips, camps, video games, computers and braces. Eventually they may want to join the ski club, go to the prom, learn to drive and buy a car, and someday finally they may head off to college. That's when the spending really kicks into high gear.

Then of course there are some of the less noticeable, but no less significant, financial impacts, like higher grocery and utility bills to name two. You may also want a bigger car, maybe a second or even a third one. The larger house soon follows. It is a spending rocket that takes off full of fuel, shooting higher and higher year after year, and which may never touch down.

For those of you who have children, I'm not telling you anything you don't already know, as you are already riding the spending rocket. For those of you without children who are considering becoming parents, consider this a warning of sorts. I am not suggesting that the decision as to whether or not to have kids should be purely based on financial considerations. What I am suggesting, however, is that the impact kids can have on your financial situation should not be taken lightly.

(Sleep Patterns Aren't the Only Thing You Need to Adjust)

One of the biggest financial mistakes young parents make is that they underestimate the financial impact of raising a family and fail to adjust their spending habits to compensate. This can be especially difficult if you were childless for an extended period of time.

People have an amazing habit of adapting to their circumstances. As such, if you are used to having extra money, chances are you have figured out how to spend much of it on things like clothes, vacations, dinners out, and cars. It can be very difficult to adjust your spending habits when suddenly faced with the dramatically increasing expenses of being a parent.

In the preceding principle, I addressed how many people make decisions simultaneously with becoming a parent that only compound the problems. For example, they conclude that they need an extra bedroom, a family room, a larger backyard, or must live in a neighborhood with better public schools. So what do they do? Just before or after having a child, they enter into another spending blockbuster, buying a bigger and more expensive house, without having given themselves an opportunity to adapt to their new spending patterns.

Another common decision people make around the time they have a child is that their car is no longer big enough, safe enough, or is just too unreliable. So they buy a new car at exactly the same time the expenses of parenthood are about to hit.

People find all sorts of reasons to spend money at the time a child arrives as well. They might be as seemingly innocent as new carpet, furniture for the baby's room, a new washing machine and dryer to clean all those baby clothes, or a DVD player for all those favorite Disney movies you will be watching over and over again. Every one contributes to and compounds the financial impact.

(The Guilt of it All)

I truly believe that 90% of personal financial difficulties people manage to get themselves into are related to emotion and only 10% related to circumstance. Children are a great example. You will undoubtedly spend more money if you have children but you don't necessarily have to spend as much as you do.

Human emotion plays an incredibly important role in the finances of parenthood. For most of us, our kids are the most important part of our lives. Nothing even comes close. We will do anything for our kids. That's the problem. Most of us will not only do anything for our kids, we will try to do everything for them.

Kids can make us lose control over our normal powers of reasoning. Emotion takes over and we do things we otherwise would never consider. If you find yourself constantly facing decisions that pit your power of reason against feelings of guilt when it comes to spending on your child, ask yourself a simple question: "Am I doing this because it's the best and right thing for my child, or am I doing it so that I feel better?" Whether it's a portable CD player or their first car, it's entirely possible that less than the best will do. In fact, many times less than the best is a better option.

(Day Care Dilemma)

After having a child, many new parents quickly make the decision that one of them is not going back to work. In my opinion, there are two factors that must be considered before making this very important decision. The first factor is the personality of the parent. Let's face it; some people are better suited to stay home and care for a child full time than others. For those who are not well suited to the task, forcing them into it may do more harm than good to both parent and child.

The second factor is money. Some parents must continue working after the birth of a child just to provide for the basic needs of their families or choose to work so that they can afford the things to which they have become accustomed. Those are personal decisions that only you can make.

If you do stay home, do not underestimate the negative financial impact this may have. Your expenses will undoubtedly be increasing at the same time your income has decreased. You may also lose valuable benefits like health insurance, meaning bigger deductions from your spouse's check to pay for them. When added to any other major financial decisions you may be making, the impact of lost wages and benefits can be devastating. You will have a difficult enough time just adapting to parenthood. Too many financial changes at the same time may be emotionally unhealthy for you, your spouse and the child.

This is not a decision that should be taken lightly. My recommendation is to continue what you were doing before you had the baby. Give yourself a chance to adjust not only to being a parent but also to your new financial situation before you make any radical decisions. You will soon know what's best for you and your child, from both an emotional and an economic perspective.

(Rational Parenting)

So if you are expecting a baby, what can you do in order to prepare for the financial adjustments to come? Unfortunately, there is no easy answer to this question. Having a child is a great trade off. You will trade your time, your privacy, your pleasures and your money. In return, you get their love. It really is a good deal.

Just be reasonable and realistic in your approach to the economics of parenting. Avoid major financial decisions immediately prior to or after having a child. Make do with what you have for a time until you have a chance to assess the impact and adjust to it. Instead of a new house, try fixing and/or remodeling the old one at first. Build on a family room, new bedroom or put in some extra storage space.

Instead of a new car right away, take the old one in and have your mechanic give it a complete overhaul and tune-up, checking all the key mechanical systems. Instead of a brand new minivan, invest in a cellular phone if you don't have one and a new set of tires.

There will be an inclination to want everything new for your baby. Resist the temptation and borrow what you can. Remember, kids can want an awful lot and most of it they really don't need. You are not a bad parent if you say no once in a while. You are doing no irreparable damage to your child, and in fact, you may be doing more good by not trying to buy everything that they want.

Stay the course for a while and concentrate all your efforts on first becoming a parent. Then focus on how to handle it all financially. Once you get past the initial phases of emotional turmoil and sleep depravation, begin your preparations and your adjustment for the years ahead. It's a long and rewarding journey. Handle it responsibly and you, your spouse and your child will all prosper.

Principle 12

Explore All Your Car Acquisition Options

There's another major spending blockbuster that can get you into deep financial trouble. Aside from a mortgage payment, the single largest monthly bill that most people have is the car payment. When you add insurance, registration, license, inspections, gasoline, oil changes, repairs, and other maintenance, cars are an incredible expense.

If you make the wrong choices when buying a car, you can put yourself in a hole, and it can be difficult if not impossible to climb out. Cars are financial land mines. You will probably never own any other asset that will cost you so much and become worth so little so quickly. Worse yet, they don't last very long, so we unfortunately need to keep perpetuating the problem of buying them over and over again.

To make it worse, car shopping and buying is not an easy thing to do. For some unknown reason long ago the process turned into an "us versus them" proposition in regards to car salespeople, and oddly enough, we have all seemed to accept it. That being said, for many, a trip to a new car showroom can be as painful and agonizing as going to the dentist.

So here we are stuck in a difficult relationship of mutual distrust. Think of it as going to a zoo where all the animals mingle freely with the visitors.

To learn more about this unique relationship, I decided that the first thing I needed to do was to get to know "the enemy." So I began studying car dealers and their often amazing sales tactics. Although I don't have any hard and fast recommendations to totally eliminate the pain associated with the new car buying process, I did come up with a few recommendations to take the edge off. Think of it as Novocain for the new car buyer.

Do Your Homework

A few months before you are ready to buy, go out and get one those new car model preview magazines or log on to one of the numerous car buying Web sites like www.cars.com. Take out a piece of paper and make a shopping list. Start with the basics. You know the major stuff like car, minivan or SUV; two or four doors; compact, mid-size or full-size car.

After your preliminary research is complete, make some initial decisions about which vehicles satisfy your requirements (foreign versus domestic), your needs (for space, functionality and fuel economy), wants (style and color), and means (cost). Just before you are ready to head out shopping, narrow your list down to no more than three to four models.

You can easily calculate estimated payments at Web sites like www.cars.com for both leasing and purchasing. When it asks you to input the price you will pay for the car, simply assume $300 over dealer invoice, which is a reasonable deal. This is essential information you must have. The last thing you want is the dealer telling you what car you can afford.

Act Like You Have Been There Before

Walk into the dealership with confidence. Approach the first salesperson you see before they have a chance to greet you, look them straight in the eye and say: "Hi I'm (insert name). Your name is? It's nice to meet you. I am not going to buy a car tonight. In fact, I will not be ready to buy for about a month or so. I'm just comparison shopping at this point and would like to look at your (insert model)." This immediately shows the salesperson that you are not intimidated by the process (even if you are) and relieves the pressure, as he or she knows that there will be no sale that night.

Master the Test Drive

Dealers love to get you behind the wheel for a test drive. But how truly useful is a 10-minute spin around the block in a brand new car?

Have you ever hopped out and said, "Wow, that was awful"? Probably not, but a test drive can still be worthwhile, and you should never hesitate to take one. Just remember, never test drive a car for the first time on the day that you think you may buy a car. Relieve the pressure up front by making it clear to the salesperson that you are comparison shopping only and have no intention of buying that day. That way you won't have to spend all your time in the car wondering how you are going to escape once the ride is finished.

Respect Your Emotions

Now, I will give you a few words of caution about new car shopping. Remember in principle 8 the discussion about the emotional gratification that comes with spending money? Be especially cautious when it comes to car shopping, as there is nothing that will get hold of your psyche and not let go more than the itch to buy a new car.

The decision to buy a new vehicle cannot be taken lightly. A little common sense and respect for the emotional implications can go a long way to keeping you out of trouble.

For example, don't visit the Mercedes lot when the only thing you can afford is a Ford. Never test drive the Lincoln Navigator if the $40 you spend at the gas pump every few days means your family doesn't eat dinner on Tuesdays.

New cars possess a remarkable power of seduction. They can draw you in and find your weaknesses. Stay within your means and most of all, stay out of the showroom unless you're absolutely convinced that you are ready and able to buy.

Consider Safety

Safety has become an increasingly important factor in the new car buying process. Keeping yourself and your family safe can go a long way toward making your life simpler. For comprehensive safety information go to the Insurance Institute for Highway Safety Web site at www.hwysafety.org. They are the independent, non-profit research organization that the insurance companies rely upon to figure out how much to charge you to insure your new possession.

There is a great deal of information out there, including results of the critically important frontal offset test. Those are the crash tests that many experts consider more realistic than head-on government tests as they simulate collisions that occur on an angle. The Insurance Institute also collects data on highway safety using actual insurance industry claims experience.

Deal with a Dealer

If you're looking to buy a new car, chances are you need to go to a dealership, right? That may have been the case in the past, but today there are plenty of alternatives available to you, the most common being the virtual showroom. You can go on the Internet to a Web site like www.autobytel.com. In the virtual showroom, there are no salespeople and there is no pressure, and that's precisely why it's so appealing to many people.

There is plenty of good information available on the Internet that will help you make an informed new car purchase. Use it to your advantage. My recommendation, however, is to stop short of actually trying to buy your car online, as Internet car shopping is all about averages.

Internet car pricing strikes a balance between people who pay a dealer too much for their car and those who pay far less. So if you are a strong negotiator, you will probably end up with a better price by going in person. If you are a poor negotiator, you may be better off using the Internet.

Internet car shopping may be impersonal, but it won't necessarily be simple. It might be pretty easy to buy things like books and toys online but not so with a new car. Provided you know what you want, have a basic understanding of how the process works and remember to keep my keys to success that we have just discussed in mind, it's really pretty easy to buy a car in person.

Don't think that buying a car on the Internet means you will never again have to talk to a car salesperson. Most services simply refer your request to a nearby dealer who takes over from there.

Know the Right Price

You have narrowed your wish list down to two models. Hold one in reserve, just in case you can't swing the right deal or get exactly what you want. Concentrate, however, on just one model at this point.

Next get yourself a copy of an Edmunds new car guide or go to www.edmunds.com. Here you will find all sorts of valuable information about the car you are looking at, including how much the dealer pays for it.

Now I'm not going to dish out a whole lot of advice on what you should pay for your car. You will find plenty of that in Edmunds and elsewhere. I will, however, offer a few simple rules to follow:

- Without considering rebates, $0-$300 over dealer invoice is generally a fair deal.

- Never shop for prices in the classifieds. Many new car ads that appear in the local newspaper are so deceptive that you are just wasting your time looking at them.

- Always tell dealers up front that you are going to comparison shop and where you plan to do so.

- Understand that dealers make additional profit if they arrange the financing for you.

- Know if you can afford the car before you ever talk price and never shop for a payment even if it's your number one concern.

Control Your Salesperson

So you have completed your homework and you are ready to buy. What should you do next? Just before the end of the month call the salesperson and inform him or her that you are ready to talk business. Give them all the details about the make and model that you want with all the options, over the phone.

Finish by saying that you have some price checking to do and that you will call back later that week.

To maintain control over the purchase process, never appear too committed to any one model or make or in a hurry to get a deal done. Wait a few days and then call the salesperson back and tell him or her what you are willing to pay (say invoice).

It's pretty certain you will get the "come on in and we can talk to the sales manager" or the "we can make a deal happen for you" speech. Keep in mind that the last thing a dealer wants to do is negotiate the sale of a car over the phone. They want you in the showroom. Over the phone, there is no commitment and nothing to make you feel guilty or embarrassed. That's exactly the idea.

If they say they do not give prices over the phone, tell them how extremely busy you are. Be persistent: "Can we do a deal at $100 over invoice, yes or no." Most dealers will eventually tell you that they can do the deal even if they do not intend to do so. If you get no promise but only generalities such as "come in and we will do our best," my advice is to stay away from that dealership.

Once they agree to your price, ask about incentives or favorable lease/financing terms. Refuse to tell them at this point whether or not you intend to lease or if you have a vehicle to trade in. Remember, the price is the price whether you lease or buy.

Close the Deal

If you are comfortable that you know exactly what model you want and that the dealer will honor the verbal commitment to sell you the car for a price you consider to be fair, set up an appointment to stop in to finalize the deal. Tell them you want the purchase contract all drawn up and ready to go, as you will have very little time.

Remember that even though you will be excited, do not appear to be too anxious. Perhaps arrive a little late for your appointment and consider taking a child with you or a disinterested companion. If things don't work out how you expect them to, these distractions give you a great excuse to bail out and leave.

Once you arrive, ask for a copy of the sales contract. Take a copy home with you and tell them you will call tomorrow. In the comfort of your home, review all the essential terms, including model and options, and verify that you are paying the price you were promised. If you are comfortable that everything is as promised, close the deal.

Leave Finances to Last

Once the price of the car is established, you can talk financing. Go to the dealership with your calculator and an impressive notebook even if you have no intention of using it. Ask that the financing and leasing terms be spelled out for you. If you are leasing, follow the techniques for negotiating an easy lease that you are just about to read. Ask who is providing the financing. It's difficult to negotiate a lease without a dealer, but loans are easy. If you are so inclined, shop the rates on your own.

Once you feel that you have all the information you need, inform the dealer of your financing decision. If you want to make sure all the numbers are in order, take the information they gave you home and log on to a Web site like www.cars.com. You can input the vital data into the loan/lease calculator to verify the payment.

Get It In Writing

Make sure all verbal commitments are written down. Not so long ago I went to pick up a new car, hopped in and noticed that the floor mats that had been promised to me were not inside. The sales manager said to me that he did not recall the mats being in the deal and that there was no indication of it in the contract. This is the same individual who had promised them to me days earlier. You can take the word of a car salesperson, as long as it is written down!

Also write on the contract that you do not want any costly dealer add-ons like fabric protection and rust proofing. What comes from the factory is all you need; don't let dealers surprise you by adding these high-profit extras without your approval.

(The Trade-In)

If you are planning to trade in your current car, about all I can say to you is good luck and be prepared to be pillaged. At www.edmunds.com, they will give you trade-in and market value information about your car. Expect that the dealer will offer you less, significantly less, than either value in most cases. Dealers make huge profits by selling used cars.

If you have a trade-in, don't tell the dealer about it until the purchase price of the new car has been agreed to and settled. Your new car purchase and old car sale should be two completely separate transactions. If you allow them to be negotiated as one, chances are you will end up with a bad deal on both ends.

When it comes to your trade-in, be prepared. The dealer will probably claim that the estimated value of your car that you have obtained over the Internet is inaccurate. Stick to your guns. If they don't give you a reasonable price, inform them that you are going to sell it on your own.

The other ploy dealers love to use is a "test drive" of your old car. Invariably, they will want to go alone. Do not let them. The drive alone in your car is a time for them to find something wrong with it. If there is anything majorly wrong with the car, be sure you know about it and tell them up front. They will find out because they are pros. You should do your homework and know what it will take to repair and replace any broken items. Remember that a car dealer will get these things done at a much cheaper price than you will; figure in their cost at 50% of yours (or less).

All that said, it is still a great idea to thoroughly clean and polish you car before taking it to the dealer. A clean, good-looking car is much more likely to bring a good price than a messy, dirty one will.

(Used Cars)

There is no doubt that you can save a lot of money by buying a good used car, especially if you avoid the dealer showroom. The problem is that finding a good used car may be a time-consuming and frustrating proposition.

I cannot dispute that from a purely economic perspective buying a used a car is usually the way to go. The most significant decrease in value is paid by the original owner, not you.

If you plan to keep a used car for only a few years and you buy a model that's less than four years old, chances are pretty good that you will have a problem-free ownership experience. However, purchasing a used vehicle can be a bit like going to the casino and playing the slots. You never know exactly what you will get. Owners who had little emotional attachment to their cars, especially if they were leased, may have abused even low-mileage cars.

One relatively new innovation has made this process just a little easier for the average consumer. Manufacturers have come up with some creative "warranty plans" to help their dealers get rid of all those low-mileage, pre-leased vehicles that were cluttering up their lots. They go by many different names but generically I will call them "certified pre-owned vehicle programs" or CPVPs. These CPVPs basically give used car buyers a greater degree of assurance that what they are buying is mechanically sound.

The exact terms differ between companies, but these programs can extend the manufacturer's warranty to as long as six years and 100,000 miles in some cases and provide additional benefits, including roadside assistance and even a money back satisfaction guarantee. Many companies will even allow you to lease these certified vehicles. Dealers are required to give the cars a thorough inspection in order to be accepted into the program.

Once accepted, the dealer will make sure that the car is in peak operating performance, may put new tires and brakes on it, change the oil, and even install new wiper blades. There is no dispute that CPVPs can go a long way toward alleviating the anxiety that often accompanies the purchase of a used car.

In fact, about the only problem with CPVPs is that dealers can sell these certified vehicles often at a substantial premium over what you will pay for a comparable vehicle that doesn't come with the same warranty protection.

It is almost always going to end up costing you less to own a used car than a new one, especially one that comes with some assurance that you will not have to pay to fix big mechanical problems. Make no mistake, however, you can overpay for a used car, just as you can a new one. Also keep in mind that you should never buy a used car without having it inspected by an independent mechanic. Regardless of the cosmetic condition or miles, have it looked at by a professional.

(Leasing Alternative)

As the price of new cars has steadily increased so too have the imaginative ways in which the manufacturers and dealers have figured out to help us pay for them. Leasing, which started out as a way for people to drive a car they could otherwise never afford, has become a widely accepted and often-preferred alternative to traditional financing.

To many, however, leasing remains as malevolent as the car salesperson. It's the secret weapon that dealers roll out on unsuspecting and uneducated buyers to ensure that the carnage is complete. To others, leasing is one of the greatest financial inventions ever and the only way that they can afford to own a new car. For most, it's just another confusing option.

(The Leasing Decision)

Some experts will tell you that leasing always costs you more and that dealers make most of their profits on leases. Others will say that leasing is the only way to go because you don't have to tie up money in a depreciating asset. Neither is consistently true.

For the vast majority of people, car buying and financing decisions simply come down to "what do I want versus what can I afford." It really doesn't matter that it may be to your economic advantage to pay $512 over 36 months to buy the car rather than $390 over 36 months to lease the car. What does matter is that "I want that car, I want it in red, and I can't afford $512 a month." This is the all too unfortunate reality, as many people use leasing to acquire cars they really cannot afford.

(Finding the Ease in Lease)

For many people, including me, the biggest advantage to leasing is that you don't actually own the car. As such, you can avoid the hassles associated with trading in your old car that I just addressed, and you avoid the other, more painful alternative of having to sell it on your own. For this reason alone, I am sold on leasing. In addition, if you lease properly you will pay for nothing more than gasoline, car washes and the occasional oil change. Your monthly car expenses are going to be basically fixed.

There are complications, however. If you don't understand the process, the dealer will have an advantage over you and may take you for more than a test ride! The initial paperwork can be intimidating, and you could pay out a considerable amount of cash up front for taxes, a down payment, etc. There can also be complications when you go to turn in the keys.

(Talk the Talk)

To help you get started and to become familiar with some of the more common "lease lingo" you will be hearing, here are some answers to commonly asked questions.

What is a lease?

Quite simply a lease is an agreement that allows you to use something that someone else owns in exchange for a fee, usually in the form of periodic monthly payments. In a way, it is like renting a car, only on a long-term basis.

How does it differ from a loan?

Banks and leasing companies loan you money to buy things. In a lease, legally you have purchased nothing. Although you negotiate the price, the leasing company is actually buying the car and you are making payments in exchange for them letting you use it.

What is the "residual" value?

The residual is the amount the leasing company estimates "their" car will be worth at the end of the lease, expressed as a percentage of sticker price. That is, what they think they can sell it for when they get it back from you. In most leases today, you will have the option to buy the car at the end of the lease term for the residual amount.

How much do I actually pay back when I lease?

Whether you lease or buy, you will be responsible for interest on the full amount of the purchase price, less any amounts you put down. The way the purchase price is paid back, however, differs significantly from a loan to a lease. Let's take a simple example.

Assume you decide to buy a car with a $23,000 sticker price. You negotiate a price of $20,000. If you take out a loan for the full amount you will repay the whole $20,000, which is known as "principal," plus interest on that amount.

If you lease that same car and you negotiate the same $20,000 price, you still pay interest on the whole purchase price but you only pay back part of principal, specifically the difference between the price you pay and the residual. You might look at this by imagining that you are financing most if not all of the down payment.

If the residual in this case is $12,000 you would pay back interest on $20,000 but principal of only $8,000 ($20,000 less $12,000 residual). This is probably more than most people ever wanted to know about leasing, and it can be confusing. What's important to know is that your lease payment is lower because you are not paying for the whole car but only for the portion of it that you are "using."

The principal factors in calculating the lease payment are the residual and something known as the money factor. How the residual is set is very important. If the lease is structured as an "open-ended lease," you are potentially liable for the difference between the actual fair market value at the end of the lease and what your residual is. Open-ended leases are not very common today. Most leases are now "closed end," meaning the finance company bears the residual risk.

What is the money factor?

As if leasing isn't complicated enough, the leasing companies thought they would further confuse you by the calling the interest rate they charge you a "money factor." To convert a money factor to an annual percentage interest rate, simply multiply it by 2400, or better yet, just insist that the dealer convert it for you.

How do I know that the payment amount was calculated properly?

The dealer and the finance manager used to have a decided advantage over the average car buyer when it came to leasing. The math is inherently complex, and most customers were not able to recalculate the monthly payment without help. This is no longer true.

With Internet access and a basic understanding of leasing, Web sites like www.cars.com make it quite simple for you to figure out exactly what your monthly lease payment will be.

By providing some basic information, you can easily calculate the monthly payment. If you have any difficulty, ask the dealer to help you. They should have a computer with Internet access right there in the showroom. Once complete, print out the payment calculations and make the dealer explain any discrepancies between your numbers and his or hers.

Make the dealer shop for the best lease. There can be big differences between interest rates and residuals, both of which can dramatically effect your payment. Never assume that the manufacturer's finance company will automatically offer the best deal.

Who is responsible for repairs and maintenance?

You are. If the car is damaged in an accident, it is your responsibility to have it repaired. You are also responsible for normal maintenance and mechanical repairs. Some people do not place a whole lot of urgency in getting routine maintenance done on a car that does not belong to them.

People who lease also commonly suffer from what I call "the rental car syndrome." Absent that pride of ownership, it is easy to neglect and mistreat a leased car. For this same reason, think twice before you ever buy a previously leased car unless there is documented proof that all required maintenance was performed as scheduled.

How long should I lease?

Today, leases are written for just about any term. I personally have had car leases ranging from as little as 27 months, which in my opinion is too short, to as long as 48 months, which is too long.

There is no right or wrong term to choose but as a general rule, never lease for longer than what the "bumper to bumper" warranty coverage period is. If you get into longer term leases of say more than 36 months, not only might the warranty coverage expire, you may also start to incur some major repair or replacement costs.

How about the miles?

A pretty standard lease contract today allows you to drive the car 12,000 miles each year over the term of the lease. Unless you know for sure that you will never come close to going over, opt for a higher mileage lease up front.

It's a whole lot cheaper than paying 15 cents for every mile you go over the limit. The joy of leasing is in not having to worry about anything, including how many miles you are racking up. If you normally drive more than 15,000 or less than 12,000 miles a year, then leasing may not be for you at all. You may be paying for the use of too little or too much car.

What about car insurance?

One thing to be aware of is that since the leasing company owns your car, they can dictate how much insurance you must carry. That is, they may require that your collision and comprehensive deductible not exceed $500 or that your liability protection not be less than $200,000. Read the contract and don't forget to factor in what may be an added expense for carrying that minimum coverage.

What is GAP insurance?

Say you are two years into a three-year lease, and your car is stolen. The finance company technically has the right to receive from you the remaining year of payments plus the residual value of the car at the end of the lease.

Well, the value of the car and correspondingly the amount the insurance company will write a check for is likely to be far less than that amount. GAP insurance, as it has been commonly known, covers the difference.

In the early days of leasing, you could buy additional insurance coverage directly from the leasing company to cover the gap. Today it's automatically built into many contracts. Make absolutely sure that your lease covers the gap if there is a catastrophic loss (your car is totaled) or your car is stolen.

Should I turn the car in at the end of the lease?

Most people just automatically give the keys back because either they do not fully understand their options or just don't want to be bothered. Remember, at the end of a lease you hold all the cards and have basically three options. You can:

- Buy the car from the finance company.
- Trade the car in if you are buying a new car.
- Turn in the keys.

Everyone seems to know that they have the option to buy the car, but most people don't seem to know that they can also trade in the car. Although legally you don't own the car, you do control all the rights of ownership.

I once turned in a Ford Explorer and got $2,000 just for asking the dealer if they were interested in purchasing it. Instead of the dealer purchasing it from the leasing company after I turned it in, they bought it from me and I got the cash.

The leasing companies have become pretty good at estimating residuals and generally you will find the car is not worth significantly more or less on trade in than the residual.

You can also try to sell the car yourself to someone other than a dealer. This can get a little tricky. Since you don't have title to the car trying to sell it before the end of the lease can be difficult. You really need to buy it from the leasing company, get the title and then sell it.

Turning the keys in and walking away from a lease is oftentimes the best thing to do, but you control the options. If the car is worth the residual or less, you just leave the problem with someone else.

Will I have a big bill at the end for damages?

We have all heard the horror stories. Your car will need to be inspected before or just after you turn it in to the dealer. Ask up front if the leasing company allows you to demand a pre-inspection report. That is, you want someone to look at your car before you turn it over so that you know what he or she thinks is wrong with it. Make sure when you do this that you get the results several weeks before you have to surrender the car so you have time to fix any problems, rather than letting them be fixed for you at the price the dealer decides is appropriate.

Make sure the details of what is considered excessive wear and tear are spelled out. You need to know up front how things like tire tread depth, stone chips, small tears in the upholstery and chips in the glass will be handled. The dealer may even try to sell you insurance to cover such costs. Remember your own insurance will pay for any major collision work. In addition, I can tell you from my own experience that if you take reasonably good care of the vehicle and have it cleaned up well before you turn it in, you should have no major problems.

Are there any other hidden costs?

All leases differ but there can be many hidden costs. The most common include acquisition fees you pay at the beginning of the lease, security deposits you pay up front and get back at the end, and disposition fees you pay when you turn in the car. Every one of these is just another way to get more out of you. Make sure all the fees are spelled out for you when the dealer quotes a payment so that you can do a fair comparison. It's possible to find leases that do not charge them, and if you ask, the dealer can often have some fees or the security deposit waived.

(The Moment of Truth)

Now it's decision time. You have picked out the make, the model and even the color. The only thing left to do is tell the dealer how you will be paying for it. Is that a lease or a buy?

You have to ask yourself honestly what it is you are trying to get out of your relationship with your automobile. Although cars are a great convenience, they can be one major and costly complication in our lives.

As with most things, there is a trade off between convenience and cost. The same generally holds true with leasing. Although not always the case, leasing can have an economic cost that is above and beyond what might be associated with a car you pay for with cash, financing with an ordinary car loan, or a used car you might buy. It's just another one of those time versus money decisions that you must make.

Principle 13
Watch Holiday Spending

Chestnuts roasting on an open fire, Jack Frost nipping at your nose; what could possibly be more wonderful than the holidays? It's the one time of the year when even the most miserable among us somehow manage to find a smile, spread some good cheer and open up our hearts and our pocketbooks.

Although maybe not on par with the other spending blockbusters, the holidays are a major spending event for most of us. Worse yet, it's not a one-time event. People do it every year, over and over again, often completely failing to recognize the problems it may be causing. In addition, retailers have recently managed to convince us that there is no longer just one major spending holiday each year but several.

(Tis the Season)

Let's focus on the major spending holiday that comes upon us each December. It seems that we have all convinced ourselves that the best way to celebrate this joyous occasion is to part with our hard-earned dollars and buy each other gifts that we don't need. The madness usually begins with the gifts for your immediate family but for many it doesn't stop there. They extend the gift list to include nieces and nephews, aunts and uncles, good friends, kids of good friends, cousins, teachers, co-workers, even the postal carrier.

Buying presents isn't the only thing that opens up your wallet during the holiday time. You will need to stock up for parties, including food, wine, beer and snacks. There are gifts for the needy, the tree, decorations, wrapping paper, cards, stamps, supplies for baking, and of course higher electric costs to power the holiday lights.

Is it possible to avoid the holiday spending trap? It is hard to avoid it entirely, but you can do a few simple things to minimize the impact. The very first thing you need to do is determine how big a trap it is. Do this by figuring out the amount of money you actually spend and more importantly, how long it takes you to pay for it all.

One easy way to keep track of things is to use your convenience card for all your purchases. Once they see all their purchases added up together in one place, most people find that their holiday spending can range anywhere from a minor financial inconvenience to a major financial disaster. Where you fall on this scale is determined by how well you have learned to control the emotion of the season and maintain a sense of reason and self-control.

(Paying the Price)

Many of us end up paying for the holidays long after the thrill of the season has faded. The tulips are out, and we're still pulling holiday bills from the mailbox. Some people go into debt for even longer periods, rolling credit cards bills into their home equity loan or juggling balances for months after the decorations have been put away.

Now, we could all simply evoke the Bah Humbug principal and just cut out or cut back on all our holiday spending. Is this realistic for most of us? Probably not, at least I know it won't work for me. Face it; most of us love to buy things during the holidays.

The holidays are a powerful time of year that can fill you with emotion. They are a time of renewal and expression for most of us. All this good feeling, however, leads many down a path of fiscal irresponsibility.

(Drawing a Line in the Snow)

So how do you minimize the impact of the holidays? To assess whether or not holiday spending may be a problem for you, ask yourself a very simply question: "How long does it take me to pay for the holidays each year?" If bills are still around in March or April, you have a problem.

There is certainly no easy solution. Most people are just not disciplined enough to control their spending. So what you must do is set yourself a dollar limit and stick to it. Draw a line in the snow and refuse to cross it no matter what the circumstances.

What should this limit be? It will be different in every circumstance but I will offer two general guidelines to consider. First, try to keep your holiday spending equal to or less than one month of "cushion" as we talked about in principle 7. Second, don't spend more than you can reasonably expect to have paid off by the end of January.

Once you draw your line, here are a few simple things you can do to help ensure that you will never cross it:

Finish Up Shopping Early

This is perhaps the single most important thing you can do. Start your shopping early and have it all wrapped up by Thanksgiving, before the real emotions of the season set in.

So what do you do during the holiday season if all your shopping is done? Try doing things you always wanted to do but never found the time to do. Take in a holiday concert, go to a school play, have people over to visit or just drive around to look at lights. There are many pleasures to be derived from the holidays that cost you nothing more than time, such as helping to package up food baskets for the needy, delivering toys to unfortunate kids, wrapping presents, or just curling up in front of the fireplace to watch *It's a Wonderful Life.*

Don't Wait in Line, Buy Online

Don't get me wrong—I'm not necessarily a big fan of shopping on the Internet. If, however, you are "challenged" by the holiday spending season, cyber-shopping may not be a bad idea, as it can help to eliminate much of the hazardous browsing that occurs when you go to the mall.

It's much more difficult to emotionally attach yourself to something you can't touch. Cyber-shopping is just less personal. It may not be quite as much fun, but in addition to helping you reduce the impulse buying urges that come with a shopping trip, it can save you an incredible amount of stress and aggravation that comes with fighting crowds.

Just Buy Fewer Presents

This is easier said than done, I know. My wife and I have tried to adhere to a rule of three major presents for our daughter, no more or no less. This is based upon the fact that baby Jesus received three major presents of gold, frankincense and myrrh. It works pretty well, and the religious aspect is an added bonus that our daughter will hopefully understand and respect as she grows older. Children are funny that way. If you simply manage their expectations, they will generally accept just about anything.

Try talking to the adults for whom you buy presents, and you may find that they are experiencing the same difficulties with buying gifts that you are. They may be all too happy to adopt a "just buy for the kids" or "don't buy for me and I will not for you" policy. Instead, spend the time enjoying good food, drink, music and the company of your friends and family rather than each other's gifts.

Remember the Emotion Fades

The best example I can think of this warning is the Furby — you know, that annoying little electronic creature that was so hot in the late 90s. People would do just about anything and pay just about any amount to get their hands on one of those little critters. It became an obsession of many a parent to get one of those prized possessions under the tree for their child.

If you were one of the lucky ones, ask yourself when was the last time your kid played with it. Now ask yourself another question. Who really wanted that Furby, your child or you? Practically every year it seems that there is some "it" item that people go crazy over buying. We have all seen the news clips of people fighting each other to grab "the prize" of the season. However, chances are that the thrill of having this item doesn't last too long and is soon forgotten. Is it really worth it?

So before you make a holiday or any purchasing decision you may regret later, try to project ahead six months in the future. Chances are whatever it may be is going to be far less important than you thought. Do you even remember half of the presents you gave to others last year?

(The True Meaning of It All)

The holidays can be a challenging time for many of us. It's important that you maintain a sense of financial reason during this challenging time of year. This is not to suggest that you ruin the moment by concentrating too much on money and too little on the real meaning of the holidays.

Get control of the financial issues before you ever enter the season. By taking a few simple steps to help control your emotions, you can push them to the back of your mind knowing that they are taken care of and under control. Before long you will realize that the holidays are about much more than spending money. There are plenty of other satisfactions that can be derived from this wonderful time of the year that do not revolve around your wallet.

Principle 14

Don't Spend Your Equity Too Quickly

Borrowing against the equity in your home is a relatively modern financial invention. Such loans come in many forms and are known by many different names. The most common is the "home equity line of credit," and it seems like today just about everyone has one.

Most people get their home equity lines from a local bank. They come with a handy little checkbook so that you can continually write checks to borrow against your equity, up to a predetermined limit, and use the money for anything you want.

Better yet, you can keep borrowing up until you reach what is known as the "repayment period." The repayment period is the specified point in time where the loan amount becomes fixed at the amount outstanding and you must start paying back what you owe. Most people never reach the repayment point, since they refinance their outstanding balance into a new line to take advantage of a lower interest rate or to borrow more.

A less common version of this same product is known as a "home equity loan." By contrast, the borrower receives a fixed amount of money up front and then pays back that amount on a predetermined schedule, just like a car loan. I will refer to them all generically as "home equity loans," even though the lines are potentially much more dangerous.

(The Loophole)

Some years back, a clever person came up with the idea to exploit our government's belief that the interest deduction on home loans is, and forever shall remain, as sacred as apple pie and the pro football blackout rule. Why not let people borrow against the value of their home to buy other things and take a tax deduction for the interest they pay? Congress and the IRS went along with it, and the floodgates were opened. The home equity loan was born.

Many consumers have greatly benefited from this creation, realizing significant tax savings, resulting from the deductibility of the interest on their home equity loans. These loans are often the most economical borrowing source available to individual consumers. That said, they can also be an inherently risky proposition.

(The Equity Trap)

Here's a pretty typical scenario to illustrate how people manage to get themselves in trouble and fall into the home equity trap:

It's a cold winter morning when you stumble outside to crank up the old Chevy — chug, chug, chug, chug…nothing. It won't start again! Frustrated, ice forming in your nostrils, you head back inside, shake the snow out from inside your shoes and proclaim, "That's it, we are buying a new car this weekend."

With a moderate sense of compassion, your spouse responds, "What about Kelly's braces and the trip to Disney World we planned for this spring? We really can't afford to buy a new car right now." What's a family to do?

You head down to the local car dealer. Before you know it, you have signed a contract to buy a limited edition Caravan. With your car as trade, you only need to come up with $24,000.

You leave the dealership with mixed emotions, happy that you will finally have a new car but uncertain as to how you are going to pay for it.

There are plenty of people who will be more than willing to help you. Just sit down and watch TV, browse some of your Internet "spam" mail, or go to the mailbox and you will see what I mean. If you own a home you can borrow money against your equity, up to $100,000 one ad says. "Wow! I only need $24,000."

It used to be that home equity lenders really cared about the value of your house. Today many lenders are satisfied if they simply know that you own the property, and they will lend you all the money you need based upon your estimate of what the house is worth or a very simple appraisal.

Traditional home equity loans, like the kind you get from your neighborhood bank, may still require lengthy applications, employment checks, appraisals, and title searches and will generally offer lower interest rates and fees than those that do not require such information. Applications that come unsolicited in the mail or by calling an 800-number you see advertised are oftentimes nothing more than high-interest personal loans disguised as home equity loans.

(Putting Some Lien on You)

Oh yes, I almost forgot the most important part. Every one of these home equity lenders will be more than happy to file a "harmless" legal document on your behalf. A document that will allow you to take a tax deduction for the interest you pay and will allow them to take your house away if you don't pay.

The fact that someone can take your house away is frightening enough, but it's not the main reason why you should proceed with the utmost of caution. Most of us are responsible enough to realize that we must keep our payments current. Home equity loans are dangerous for other reasons. Let's go back to our friends and the new Caravan to find out why.

The couple decides to stop by the local bank to check out car loan rates. "Have you considered a home equity loan?" the friendly loan officer asks. "The rate is lower than a car loan, and the interest is tax deductible." Our minivan buyers hesitate at the thought of having a second mortgage, but the lure of a tax deductible car loan is just too much to resist. A week later, they leave the bank office holding a $30,000 line of credit and a checkbook that allows them to access virtually all of the equity in their house with a stroke of the pen.

(Wrecking Ball)

Virtually everyone who takes out a home equity loan does so with the best of intentions. Our minivan buyers are no exception. They walk out of the bank convinced that they will never use that line for anything but that new minivan and that they will pay it all back over the same 48-month period they would have taken for the car loan. They received a lower rate, and the interest is tax deductible. What could possibly be wrong?

As well intentioned as you may be, that checkbook is simply too much of a temptation for many people. Do yourself a favor and hide it. That checkbook is like a package of Oreos sitting on the bedside table of a chocoholic on a diet. Sooner or later you will probably find justification for opening the bag.

Regardless of your original intent, it's very easy to convince yourself to use the loan and justify it based upon the tax deductibility of the interest. For many, it's this feature that allows them to rationalize spending what they might not otherwise consider. When combined with the extended repayment schedules, home equity loans can be a personal financial wrecking ball if not used responsibly.

The excuses for tapping into your equity are varied and convincing:

- I want to get all my credit cards consolidated into one payment.

- I still owe on my old car but really need a new one. I'll take out a loan for the new car and pay off the balance of the old loan with the home equity.

- It's for my child's education.

- We really need a vacation.

- Why shouldn't I get a tax deduction for all that interest?

- It's my equity, and I intend to spend it.

Proceed with caution because a home equity loan offers just too many opportunities to fall in the trap.

(The Pay Off)

Our minivan buyers write the check for the $24,000 purchase price and each month religiously pay back an amount equal to what the car payment would have been. Then the inevitable happens. They find a reason not to make a full payment.

Remember, because of the extended payment terms, the required monthly payment on the home equity loan will be very small, even if you have a large balance outstanding. It takes discipline, and a lot of it, to pay more than the minimum payment that is required. The real test is if you can keep it up for the long haul, especially those months when unexpected expenses occur.

It takes even more discipline not to add to your outstanding balance by paying for things other than what was originally intended. Once you do that, your balance becomes fungible and for all but the most disciplined, the battle is lost. It's no longer a car loan or an education loan but merely a loan.

(Lost Equity)

Not everyone will succumb to the trap, but it can be very difficult to avoid. Many home equity borrowers find themselves paying for things like cars and vacations over 20 years. The additional interest they end up paying may far exceed the tax benefit and may be four or five times the original cost.

Remember, no matter how harmless it seems, you have another lien attached to your house, and home equity lenders can become very aggressive if you don't or can't pay.

Unless you used your loan to pay for a major remodeling project or an addition to your house that added value, spending your equity can leave you with nothing but a large unpaid mortgage. Just remember your home equity loans must be repaid when you sell your house. Many people become trapped because they cannot come up with the down payment or closing costs on a new home after they pay off all the home equity.

(Safety Tips)

A home equity loan can have financially devastating effects if not handled with care. Unfortunately, they don't come with instruction manuals. So if you have or are considering getting one, keep these rules of safe operation in mind at all times:

- Try to avoid using your home equity to pay for things you will quickly consume and that produce no tangible future benefits (for example: vacations, holiday spending, weddings and parties, car repairs).

- Do not extend payments beyond what they would have been with a conventional loan. If you buy a car with your home equity, pay it back over four or five years.

- Consider a home equity *loan* with its fixed principal amount and repayment schedule rather than a far more dangerous line of credit.

- Make it difficult to vary from your originally intended repayment schedule by setting up automatic payments.

- Don't use your home equity to pay off existing debts that will free up your emotional line of credit.

- If you have a line of credit, limit access to your checkbook that accompanies it.

- Avoid rolling one unpaid home equity loan into a new, bigger loan.

- Remember that a tax deduction is nice, but it does not provide justification for spending money.

The ideal situation is to have a home equity loan, specifically a line of credit, but never use it. Why bother? As you will read later, there's a funny thing about credit. You get plenty of it when you have no use for it, but when you do need it, it's hard to find. Think of it as a free insurance policy.

(Stiff Competition)

You can explore home equity options at Web sites like www.e-loans.com, but you want to consider sticking with traditional lenders like your neighborhood bank or credit union, provided that their rates are resonably competitive. Virtually all lenders now offer low introductory and competitive long-term interest rates and no fees or closing costs. Avoid the solicitations that arrive in your mailbox or that you hear about on late night television. The approval process may be a bit more time consuming at your bank, but the rates are often better.

In addition, many traditional home equity lenders still follow strict guidelines that make it impossible for you to borrow or spend all of your equity. Also, remember that little piece of paper that was filed on your behalf, known as the lien? If you get into unexpected trouble down the road, it's nice to have a fellow member of your community holding it, someone with a local reputation to protect.

Treat the equity in your home with the respect that it deserves. It takes a long time to build this most valuable asset; be careful not to squander it.

Principle 15
Be Your Own Lender

You have reached the point where you just can't take it any more, all those sleepless nights, tossing and turning in your bed, worrying about where the money is going to come from to pay the bills. Tuition is due next month, car insurance next week, the house needs a new roof, you need some new clothes, you could all use a vacation, and the holidays are just around the corner. You have been carrying balances on your credit cards for years, and the prospects for paying them off seem all too remote. What you need is a little infusion of cash, but where can you get it?

(The Options)

There are those "checks" you receive in the mail. You know, the ones that you open because they look as if they could be from the IRS. Then you tear open the envelope only to discover that they are nothing more than applications for high-interest personal loans. Then, of course, there are the home equity loans we addressed in the last principle. Often disguised with names like "debt consolidation" or "personal equity" loans, they are every financial advisor's solution to your financial problems.

Credit cards are always an option, right? Although I am not absolutely opposed to using a credit card as a source of borrowing, it surely is not a preferred, long-term solution. Well-selected and well-managed credit cards can be an attractive borrowing alternative but handling them properly requires time and energy.

(Turn to the Bank of You)

Despite recent setbacks, the meteoric rise in the stock market during the 1990s has left many folks with the unique opportunity to function as their very own bank. Sitting on appreciated nest eggs in their tax deferred, employee sponsored retirement accounts or "401(k) plans," the cash may be there for the asking.

If you have a 401(k), many employers allow you to loan money to yourself, pay it back to yourself, and best of all, keep all the interest. On top of that, your employer will take your loan payments directly out of your paycheck, so you will never have the opportunity to develop an emotional attachment to the money or stretch your payments over a longer period of time than you originally intended.

(The Sacred Cow)

Ask any traditional financial advisor and most will tell you that borrowing from your 401(k) is simply a bad idea. You will probably hear things like: "You are spending the future"; "Retirement savings are sacred, never touch them"; or "It doesn't make economic sense." I must admit, during the peak of the stock market run, even I was almost convinced that maybe it didn't make sense to touch your invested retirement savings. However, now that we all know the market can go down as well as up, I am perplexed by the outright objections people continue to have against borrowing their own money. It seems that these objections are based more upon conventional wisdom than upon true wisdom. Just answer the following question and you will begin to see what I mean.

What would you rather do?

  A. Borrow $10,000 from someone else and pay them $1,000 interest.

  B. Borrow $10,000 from yourself and pay yourself $1,000 interest.

The answer seems all too obvious. Under scenario B, you will end up with $1,000 more in your pocket. Is it always better to pay interest to yourself than it is to pay interest to someone else? No, but let's start with the basics.

When you take out a loan against your 401(k) account, you are borrowing your own money. Not only does the federal government allow you to put money into these accounts without paying any taxes until you start withdrawing the money at retirement age, they also allow you to spend that money on anything you want, tax and penalty free. All you have to do is pay it back to yourself, with interest that *you* get to keep.

There is a big emotional hurdle to clear when it comes to "spending" your retirement money. "That's the retirement money! If I touch that I'll end up dependent on my children. No way am I spending it!"

Although it's generally not a good idea to spend your retirement nest egg before you retire, don't rule out a 401(k) loan just yet. Remember that you must pay the money back. There are no negotiations, no missed payments and no exceptions. You decide up front over what period of time you wish to repay, tell your employer, and they do the rest.

There is only one very bad feature about borrowing from your 401(k). If you leave your job, voluntarily or not, the loans are immediately due and payable. If you are laid off, such an obligation couldn't come at a worse time.

If you don't or can't repay, the loan is considered a premature distribution and taxed as income to you in the year received, and there is a 10% premature distribution penalty on top of it. As you will read later on, there are preparations you can make for that possibility too, so this feature should not render 401(k) loans an unviable option.

(The Analysis)

Please accept my apology for the level of detail you will find in the analysis that follows. This is an important topic, however, and one that receives so much negative press that I felt compelled to provide it for the benefit of those who still need to be convinced that borrowing from your 401(k) just may not be such a bad idea. If you take my word for it, just skip right by it.

Assume you have a $10,000 balance in your 401(k) and you need a $10,000 loan. You have two options. Either borrow $10,000 from yourself or borrow the $10,000 from someone else. Assume you will pay $1,000 of interest on either loan so the amount of cash out of your pocket will be $11,000 in both cases.

How much will you have left if you borrow from someone else?

Answer: $10,000

You will still have the original $10,000 in your 401(k) and will have paid $11,000 to whomever loaned you the money.

How much will you have left if you borrow from yourself?

Answer: $11,000

Since you are paying yourself, you will have the entire $11,000 you repaid in your 401(k).

This is an overly simplified example as it assumes no earnings on the 401(k). It does, however, illustrate the basic concept.

Now, let's go a step further and assume you borrowed the $10,000 from someone else and left the money in your 401(k) account where it earned $500.

How much would you have left?

Answer: $10,500

You would have paid $11,000 to whomever you borrowed from and have $10,500 in your 401(k) representing the original balance plus the $500 in earnings. In this case you would have been ahead borrowing from yourself, since the interest you paid to whomever you borrowed from exceeded the amount earned on the funds by $500.

Remember the equation? Here's another way to look at it. Say you take out a tax deductible home equity loan for four years to buy a car, and the interest rate you pay (after tax) is 5%. How can you beat that low rate?

Let's say the stock market continues to lag, and the money you left in your 401(k) only earns 2% after tax. That tax deductible home equity just cost you 3% per year. You would have been better off taking the money for your car out of your 2% investment than paying 5% interest to someone else.

You only need to remember one thing. It's impossible to figure out whether or not it makes economic sense to borrow from yourself in advance of making the decision, unless you have psychic powers or a crystal ball that allows you to accurately predict how much your 401(k) investments will earn.

So unless you are investing your 401(k) money in some type of investment with a guaranteed return, all this analysis is relevant only with the benefit of hindsight. If you are getting a guaranteed return, chances are the amount you are earning is going to be less than any external borrowing cost.

Concerned about the interest rate on your 401(k) loan? Remember, the interest rate is relevant only from a cash flow perspective. You are paying this interest to yourself so do not be concerned if the rate on your 401(k) loan exceeds the rate on some other source of borrowing. It's only the rate on the loan in comparison to the return on the invested money that matters.

Oh sure, the experts who tell us that borrowing your retirement money is a bad idea all looked pretty smart when the stock market was roaring ahead every year with double-digit gains, but in today's market, it's a whole different story. So if you find yourself in need of cash, especially for a short-term period during which market returns are far less than predictable, stop agonizing over the decision and consider giving yourself a loan.

Principle 16
Investigate Equity Investments

We have now all seen the evidence; investing in stocks can truly be a risky business. Some are better equipped than others to deal with the ups and downs of market investing; they have a higher tolerance for risk. Over the past several years, however, even the most sensitive of investors had been lulled into a false sense of security, believing that the market moves only in one direction and all but forgetting the inherent risks associated with investing.

It's important to remember that all stock market performance, like the weather, is only temporary. If you don't like it today, check tomorrow, next week or next year perhaps, and chances are that it will be entirely different. The "experts" will tell you that over time there is no better investment vehicle than the US equity market. I cannot dispute this. The long-term performance of the stock market in general is unmatched, as is its irrational behavior.

In the months preceding the big plunge of 2000, the stock market gurus appearing on nightly business shows proclaimed tech stocks traded on the NASDAQ exchange "the Dow of the future." The old economy stocks and industries were dying on the vine, they said. High-speed fiber optic cables were quickly replacing smokestacks, and it was no longer considered "cool" to make cars and power tools.

Fast forward and now we all know that the NASDAQ can and has "corrected," and the companies of the old school Dow, although certainly having taken some lumps, have not gone away. Those same experts now tell us that tech stocks may have been valued more on potential than on actual results.

More recently, we have learned about the profound impact that a large-scale national tragedy can have on the economy and stock prices. In addition, we have learned that scandals and corruption within corporations can have a big impact on investors' wallets.

(Riding the Market)

So what does all this mean? It means that the stock market is the tallest, fastest and most dangerous roller coaster ride in the world. It will go up; it will go down. Maybe it stays down for a few days in a row or maybe for a week, a month, a few months or even a few years. Sometimes it goes up and down several times during the same day.

What is more amazing is that on different days it will interpret the same information in different ways. It all depends on the mood. You see, the market and those who invest are many things, but one thing they are not is rational.

(Building a Pyramid)

All this irrational behavior will hopefully not scare you away from market investing. For it would be in our collective best interest to ignore everything and just continue to pour our money into stocks. You see, whether we realize it or not, the stock market has become the greatest pyramid scheme the world has ever known.

During the late 1990s, many of us discovered that we could make a whole lot of money doing absolutely nothing. For those fortunate enough to jump into the fray, we have been the beneficiaries of some pretty incredible market returns.

So how did it all work? It's really pretty simple. As the stock market continued to post incredible returns, it quickly became the stuff of which legends were made. Everyone was talking and, more importantly, pouring more and more of their savings dollars into individual stocks, mutual funds, and retirement funds.

That is, we kept feeding the bottom of the pyramid, and when that happens, it keeps growing and everyone benefits.

Investors have for the most part learned to keep their senses about them, understanding that if they bail out, the pyramid will collapse and the machine stops printing money.

So if you are already in the market and have no immediate need for the invested cash, consider sticking with it. If you are thinking of joining in, prepare yourself to accept the inevitable consequences of market investing.

Expect the unexpected, and expect that on occasion what happens will make you wish that you had never decided to become involved. Approach market investing with the caution that it deserves.

(It's Not for Everyone)

As you have been reading, so much of our personal finances revolve around emotion. One key to simplification is learning to master your emotions about money, which allows you to make decisions that ultimately help you control your financial destiny. Unfortunately, an investment in the stock market can be both extremely uncontrolled and highly emotional.

Although there are steps you can take to minimize the impact, assess your personality and financial situation carefully before you decide whether or not the stock market is right for you. You must assess your tolerance for risk and the impact it will have on you emotionally. If you are not the type of person who can look the other way and deal with it rationally, then the potential returns you are giving up may not be worth the emotional turmoil you will suffer. Just as you avoid the casino if you are not prepared to lose, you should likewise avoid the market.

(Market Rules)

Most of us can actually manage to strike up a comfortable relationship with the emotionally troubled market. Just understand that you are dealing with an irrational force. In this regard, here are a few basic rules of market investing that I always try to keep in mind:

- ï Be prepared to lose money.

- ï Accept that the market is nothing more than a conglomeration of emotionally unstable and confused investors who will behave irrationally.

- ï Set a strategy and stick with it.

- ï Avoid looking at performance on a short-term basis.

- ï Ignore the experts, especially just after any large market movement.

- ï If you buy individual stocks, look for companies that sell things that we always need under any circumstances, like groceries and pharmaceuticals.

- ï Remember that market investing is just like gambling with one major difference. Over time, history has proven that you should end up winning.

The key to stock market success is generally "time," not only the time you must be willing to invest in all the research necessary to succeed but also the length of time you are willing to wait for your return. If you pick stocks with care, follow a regimen of knowing when to buy and when to sell, do your homework, and are prepared to wait, you will probably do okay. Unfortunately, statistics show that despite the enormous cumulative increase in the market from 1990 onward, most investors only yielded about 6% annual return, and despite their skill and training, experts averaged only 12%. It is definitely not a get-rich-quick proposition. However, for those willing to invest the time and the money, it can be rewarding.

(Market Strategies)

Let's assume that you are in fairly reasonable physical, emotional and financial health. Should you get on this ride or not? It's a really difficult question to answer, especially today, and one that people seem to be asking more often than any other. Normally my response is in the form of a question. What's your objective? Most people will respond with something like "to maximize my return" or simply "to make money."

Next I ask them specifically, "Over what period of time are you looking to do this?" If the answer is 10 years or less, I generally instruct them to steer clear of the market.

Everyone wants a safe market strategy, and it simply does not exist. If safety is what you are looking for, then your strategy should be to simply avoid the market. Here's my personal market strategy, and it's a relatively simple one. Basically, every dollar of my retirement savings in my 401(k) plan is 100% invested in the market, even today. Virtually every other dollar I save outside of my 401(k) plan is invested in anything but the stock market, primarily short-term market rate investments.

I hold a few individual stock investments, but that's really only for the fun of it. My recent experiences with these stocks, however, have caused me to reconsider just how much fun it really is. As I near retirement, I will inevitably begin shifting those retirement funds to cash as well.

My strategy has developed because of my inability to tolerate the emotional ups and downs of short-term market investing. I hardly ever look at the balance in my 401(k) account, and when I do, I have very little concern over what it is doing since the time frame is long term. When it comes to my personal non-retirement savings, the money I can spend today, it just hurts too much to see it disappear.

Will I become independently wealthy following this strategy? Probably not, but I sleep well at night. I have made an investment decision that is right for me. Having weighed the options, I decided to sacrifice some potential return for simplicity and peace of mind. Should you do the same? Well, only you can decide that. Regardless of your decision, just keep it simple. Set an investment philosophy and stick with it. Limit the number of accounts you have and don't over-manage by reacting to short-term positive or negative market movements.

(Mutual Funds)

There is a common misconception that much of the pain associated with market investing can be avoided by sticking with mutual funds. Long viewed by the average investor as the easiest, most cost-effective way to build a diversified portfolio, these funds offered virtually everyone the opportunity to get in on the action, with little knowledge, experience or time commitment necessary.

Even small investors could build handsome portfolios over relatively short periods of time. All you need to do is write out a check, and the expertise of some of the most powerful fund managers in the world could be working for you. The myth has now been all but shattered.

(Search for the Best)

What could be easier than mutual fund investing? We have all seen those annual rating and preview guides that show up in supermarket checkout lanes. They usually picture a slightly graying couple on the cover dressed in matching sweaters with confident smiles on their faces telling the world, "Our family is secure forever thanks to the outstanding performance of some well-selected mutual funds."

The headline generally reads something like: "The Ultimate Annual Mutual Fund Review," "The Five Hottest Funds," or "Where to Invest $5,000 Today." Just add them to your shopping cart and they are sure to provide you with enough information to make you just as happy as that artificial couple on the cover.

(Complex Numbers)

If you have never actually purchased one of these magazines be forewarned that although they contain a lot of good information, they are not always simple to follow and understand. You will generally find the ratings divided into fund categories like "Stock Funds," "Bond Funds," "Sector Funds," "Indexed Funds," "Growth Funds," "Income Funds," "Growth and Income Funds," "Capital Appreciation Funds, "Emerging Markets Funds, "European Funds," "Precious Metals Funds," and so on.

In a recent mutual fund annual review published by a major personal finance magazine, there were some 23 pages devoted to stock funds alone. There were close to 2,000 funds on those pages, all with little different colored arrows, half-moons inverted, and upright triangles next to them, attempting to explain to me how good or bad they were.

As you turn the pages, you might just feel as if you have discovered the ruins of an ancient city and come upon walls inscribed with some complex series of symbols that surely hold the key to a lost civilization. The problem is how to break the code. Not knowing where to begin, you might start with the top 10 list. How can you possibly go wrong by just picking the best performing fund and going with it?

(Scientific Experiment)

To answer this question, I decided to do a little research. I logged on to one of my favorite personal finance Web sites, www.smartmoney.com, and went to the mutual funds tab. There I found just about every piece of information I ever wanted to know about mutual fund performance.

You can review the performance of more than 6,000 funds for periods ranging from one day to five years. So I set out to determine what the best performing funds were. I started out with a one-year performance for all funds. It came back with a list of 25 top funds ranked by annualized returns.

I then proceeded to check the five-year performance period for all funds. It quickly produced another list of 25 funds that again were ranked by annualized returns.

Much to my surprise, not one fund appeared on both lists. Given the recent collapse of the equity markets, it seemed that many precious metals funds had made their way into the list of top performers. So in the interest of fairness, I decided to conduct the same experiment using a more comparable group of funds. Selecting mid-cap growth equity funds, I again listed the best 1- and 5-year performers. Once again, no fund appeared on both lists. It seems that top performing funds could not deliver consistent results. All I wanted was the "best" mutual fund.

The answer is not easy to find. Those magazines in the checkout lines were focused on short-term results rather than the more important long-term qualities, like the ability of the fund to control expenses and weather turbulent markets. Don't think you are automatically going to find the "best" funds just by looking at this year's top 10 list. Stock market investing should be viewed as a marathon race, not sprint. Many funds are good sprinters but they don't always hold up for the long haul.

(So Many Options)

One of the biggest problems with mutual fund investing is that there are just too many choices. The choices are so diverse and the advice on selecting the "right" funds so plentiful that it's easy to become lost and confused. More importantly, mutual funds can lead you down the path toward complexity. Who hasn't looked at one of those magazines and thought, "Maybe I should put some money into that hot fund."

In the past, people generally chased funds that posted the biggest returns. Now they may chase funds that show the smallest losses. None of this chasing is healthy, and before you know it, you will find yourself with funds spread out in a myriad of different accounts and swimming in a sea of complex redemptions and unwanted tax implications.

(In Control)

Any situation where you fail to control your own destiny will at best be uncomfortable and will at worse be unacceptable.

When it comes to mutual funds, you are placing your unconditional trust in someone else. You trust them to make the right investment decisions, you trust them to control their expenses, and you allow them to control your tax liabilities. This control can be hard to give up, especially when you are dealing with your money.

There are some other very good reasons for stopping to pause before you decide to mail off your check to a mutual fund:

ï   They are not necessarily tax efficient. The fund "distributes" its gains to be taxed on individual shareholder returns at the end of the year. The shareholder has no control over what tax consequences may be.

ï   The fund may have high expenses, some of which are hidden and all of which eat away at any gains.

ï   The funds are typically managed by people who have a short time frame since their bonuses are determined annually.

ï   Very seldom is the return that a shareholder receives equal to that which a fund advertises it obtained.

On the other hand, there is a lot to be said for a good, balanced mutual fund. If you choose a good, well-managed fund that holds expenses down, it's very possible that you could earn far more than the market averages. The problem is that you are going to have to choose a good fund and stick with it for the long term.

To be successful at choosing mutual funds, you will either have to rely upon a stockbroker or other commissioned financial salesperson, read the financial magazines, or spend some time on the Internet at one of the many excellent Web sites like www.smartmoney.com.

Mutual funds are not the easy investment most people think they are. You can spend a tremendous amount of time doing research and analysis trying to select the right one.

If you are buying and selling, there can be a significant record-keeping burden, which can add up to a great deal of time. You may also have complex and unwanted tax consequences. Furthermore, it's only human nature to want the best. If you are constantly chasing the "top" funds, you might end up with a complex mess on your hands.

(Investigate Other Equity Investments)

If mutual funds are not the answer, maybe individual stocks are. Unfortunately, the research necessary to build and maintain a successful individual stock portfolio can be far greater than what is required for mutual fund investments. That being said, individual stock investments do have some decided advantages over mutual funds.

For one thing, you have more control over your destiny. It's your decision to buy and sell an individual stock within your portfolio. You control your tax liabilities. If you don't want any taxable gains or tax deductible losses, you simply hold them.

Individual stocks can also be high on what I call the fun factor. It can be exciting to own the stock of a favorite or high-exposure company. I find that individual stock ownership can be a great escape mechanism. We can live out our fantasies by becoming a partial owner of companies like Microsoft (MSFT) or Disney (DIS).

Owning individual stocks has recently become much easier on the pocketbook as well, thanks to the explosion of low-cost Internet trading available on many Web sites, such as www.brokerage.us.hsbc.com. It's not all that unreasonable to think you might go online and pick up 10 or even fewer shares of your favorite company. Stock ownership has become affordable for everyone.

Individual stocks can play a useful part in the portfolio of any investor. So if you opt for this alternative, here are a few rules that I suggest you try to follow to keep your experience as simple and rewarding as possible:

ï   Be prepared to lose money.

ï   If you don't understand what the company does, avoid the stock.

ï   Never buy stock based upon information you read about in the newspaper or hear on TV. Sophisticated investors knew it before you did.

ï   Watch trends in analysts' recommendations. If you go to a site like www.smartmoney.com and enter a stock symbol, you can click on a tab labeled "Ratings." It allows you to enter different time periods to see how the professional analysts who follow the stocks and issue recommendations change over time. Don't concentrate on the current ratings so much but more on trends, such as a gradual migration in positive analyst ratings.

ï   Watch insider activities. This is the buying and selling of people who have a relationship with the company. These people are in the know. Follow their lead. You can find this information on almost any Web site that gives you detailed stock information.

ï   Don't buy a stock unless you are prepared to hold it for at least a year.

ï   Try to avoid looking at price too often during the first month you own it.

Of course, many people have become very rich by not following these rules. That's not the point. You will probably never make the cover of *Money* magazine but you should have reasonably successful investment results and, most importantly, more time on your hands to devote to the things in life that really can make you truly rich.

(The Law of Averages)

If you are searching for a diversified stock investment alternative that can be purchased with little or no research, consider an old stand-by, the indexed mutual fund.

Most of us have heard of indexed mutual funds, probably the most famous one being the Vanguard 500 Index Fund (VFINX), which invest in stocks that comprise the Standard and Poor's 500 Index. The objective is to match the exact return of the index.

As a result of this objective, the investment manager has very little discretion with regard to which investments to make. Accordingly, index funds tend to have low-expense ratios and traditionally distribute fewer of those problematic capital gains than "normal" non-index mutual funds do.

Another nice feature of index funds is that the indices themselves are comprised of various individual stocks in a wide range of industries. Investing in the index is in and of itself a somewhat diversified investment strategy.

(More than Just a Girl's Best Friend)

There is another option that is relatively new to the market known as the Exchange Traded Fund or ETF. Say for example you wanted to own a share of every individual stock that comprises the Dow Jones Industrial Average. You could go out and buy each one for about $10,000 and pay more than $1,000 in brokerage commissions. Clearly this is not a practical alternative.

You could go buy a Diamond, not the precious gemstone but one of the new breed of investment products available to investors, especially those looking to keep things simple. Similar to indexed mutual funds, Diamonds (DIA) are ETFs or individual shares of funds that invest in the stocks that comprise the Dow Jones Industrial Average.

Diamonds work more like individual shares than mutual funds do. That's because gains and losses are generally realized by investors buying and selling them and not because the fund manager sells them in order to raise cash to redeem shares. Like indexed funds, their market price tracks the net asset value of the stocks that comprise the underlying index, and fund expenses are extremely low.

Just like when you buy any shares, however, you will pay a brokerage commission each time you buy and sell an ETF. This can be a big disadvantage from no-load indexed mutual funds, especially if you are making small investments frequently. Remember, however, you can buy most ETFs through your discount or online broker, keeping those commissions very low. For those of you with day-trading tendencies lurking in your persona, ETFs can also be bought and sold all day long just like ordinary shares and unlike mutual funds that are bought and sold at closing prices each day.

(Do the Math)

Feeling especially lucky and thinking about getting into tech stocks but don't have the time or confidence to pick individual shares? You could consider buying a Qube. That's an ETF that gives you an ownership interest in the "top" 100 shares in the NASDAQ.

Spiders (SPY) are ETFs tied to the S&P 500. You can also buy Webs, which track indices in various foreign countries and all start with the symbol EE. If sector investing is more your style, there are plenty of choices including ETFs tied to the S&P MidCap (MDY), S&P Energy (XLE), and S&P Industrial (XLI).

You can make small-dollar investments in diversified portfolios across various domestic and international equity market indices, while not sacrificing all of the control that comes with individual stock ownership. Although ETFs can also distribute capital gains like mutual funds, they are generally very tax efficient so you shouldn't be in for any big tax surprises.

Just keep in mind that owning ETFs, like indexed investing, is basically playing the averages. You won't be realizing the big gains that might be associated with individual stocks, but you will also avoid some of the big losses. Make no mistake — you can do quite well by playing the averages.

ETFs can be another attractive option for the investor who is looking to diversify an investment strategy but who lacks the time, energy and resources to put together an individual portfolio. The added flexibility and low probability for tax surprises can make them an excellent choice.

(Take Stock)

We are not all suited to riding giant, high-speed, looping roller coasters. Make no mistake, the stock market is one great big thrill ride. If you decide to hop onboard, get ready. Do not underestimate the emotional and practical realities of your decision as to whether or not to participate. Do not overestimate your ability to withstand the emotional and practical realities of your decision or your ability to withstand the ups and downs. If you decide to give it a try, know your limitations, assess your appetite for adventure, decide how much time you are willing to spend in search of a thrill, and most of all, fasten your seatbelt and hold on!

Principle 17

Don't Get Crazy About College Savings

You probably began thinking about college the first day you laid eyes on your little bundle of joy. I can remember even before that looking at an ultrasound image and uttering something to my wife about our "future university graduate." We all hope and dream that our children will someday grow up to be well-educated and productive members of society. We push them to try harder and do better, to seek success and deplore failure. We want them to be everything we are and much, much more.

(Simply the Best)

Part of the dream we weave for our children almost always includes success in the classroom and on the field of play. We want them to be doctors, lawyers, engineers, dentists, quarterbacks, golfers and gymnasts. We dream that they will graduate at the top of their high school class then go on to Harvard, Yale, Stanford or Notre Dame.

The outcome is often very different from the dream. Only a handful of our kids will excel at athletics and less than 50% of them continue on to four-year colleges after graduating high school. Now you could sit back and play the odds that your child will be one of those who never goes on to college but most of us won't. Rather, we will assume that our kids will become everything we want them to be and more.

(Footing the Bill)

When it comes to college, both parents and children feel the stress of high expectations. Many parents impose significant pressure on themselves to pay for the costs of higher education, believing it is their moral and ethical obligation to do so. Others believe that if their child wants to attend college, they should pay for it on their own. Then we have the parents somewhere in between, wishing they had the ability to pay for college but uncertain if they will ever have the means to do so.

Just as our attitudes toward paying for college can be vastly different, so too can the preparations we make for it. Some turn college funding into an obsession. They save early and often, perhaps starting the day the child is born. Money is meticulously set aside each month, savings bonds are purchased, education IRAs opened, birthday and Christmas money stashed away with the single goal of paying for college.

Then there are parents who do little or nothing until just before the time comes to pay the first tuition bill. They are the ones who join the mad scramble each year to find student loans, scholarships, grants and universities offering the lowest tuition and the highest amount of financial aid.

If you are like most people today raising a young family or just starting out, I'm guessing there are a few more important things on your financial mind than paying for college tuition — how about paying the car payment, the mortgage, the phone bill and buying groceries to name a few. Although it may always be there in the back of their minds, many people manage to avoid giving much serious consideration to the matter until just about when their kids reach high school.

Failing to save for higher education can make you feel worse than not saving for retirement. After all, if you don't save for your retirement, it's you who will have to eat macaroni and cheese six nights a week, but if you don't save for college, it's your child who will suffer, destined for a dead-end job.

(The Education Maze)

As you know by now, I have made every effort to steer clear of the agonizing detail that you normally find in books about personal finance, instead offering you practical alternatives to the traditional ways of thinking about and dealing with common financial concerns. As I began to think about what recommendations I was going to make relative to saving for and financing college, however, I quickly realized that I would be remiss if I did not at least try to give you some basic information to help guide you through this complex maze of education finances.

Education IRAs

The first thing you may encounter in the maze is the simplistic tax-deferred EIRA (Education Individual Retirement Account). It's practically impossible to talk about saving money for college and not mention taxes. I have never been one to worry too much about the tax consequences; however, my primary concern has always been to avoid tax complications.

This is not to suggest that you should pursue strategies that ignore tax consequences. Taxes should always be put in perspective. An assessment should be made as to how significant the tax implications are and a decision made accordingly. Doing things that are tax wise is not always the best or easiest way to do them. An EIRA is a perfect example of that idea.

With recent tax changes, you now will be allowed to put up to $2,000 a year in an EIRA for each child you have. That's a big improvement from the whopping $500 that it used to be. Although you get no deduction on your current tax return for the contribution, the earnings on the invested cash accumulates tax free provided that you use the money to pay for school. You can even use it to pay tuition for elementary and secondary schools. The amount you may contribute phases out if you make above a certain income limit, but that will not come into play for most people.

(Drop in the Bucket)

To see how far that $2,000 was going to take you, I decided to do a little research using something called the "college cost calculator" at www.fidelity.com, where I discovered that the current average cost of attending a private university was $22,230 per year. If I wanted to start saving today for a one-year-old child to attend such a university, assuming a reasonable return on investment, you would need to put away about $337 each month the first year, then increase it monthly by an amount equal to the percentage of increase in tuition each year.

In either case, that $2,000 a year you can sock away in an education IRA is not going to get the job done. So am I suggesting that you look a proverbial gift horse in the mouth and forego the benefits of the education IRA?

Yes, as you will read, there are better ways to go. Remember, even at $2,000, you are not getting a tax deduction for the contribution but only deferring tax on the investment earnings. Also remember, if your child ends up not using the money for college, you will pay all the taxes due on the earnings plus a hefty penalty.

Saving Money in the Child's Name

Another tax savvy college savings strategy that you will often hear touted is to save money in your child's name. Not only can you force the child to stash away his or her money, but you can also add to it by giving your child an annual gift of up to $10,000 per parent without paying any gift tax. This, of course, assumes that you actually have an extra $10,000 to give to your kid. As long as the child's income from investments stays below $1,400, the tax savings can be significant as your child is generally taxed at a significantly lower rate than you are.

So that being said, is saving money in your child's name the answer? No, there is a big negative associated with this strategy. In order for it to work, the money you invest for your child must really belong to your child. This means that they have the right to spend it on anything they want when they reach the age of majority, which in most states is 18. That includes financing a tattoo parlor or buying a new sports car, and there is nothing you can legally do about it.

You may also end up having to prepare tax returns for your child. It's bad enough that you have to do your own. On top of all that, money saved in your child's name counts more heavily against you when it comes time to apply for financial aid.

State Sponsored Tuition Savings Plans

A recent addition to the education maze is the state sponsored college savings programs, also known as "529 plans." These plans are tax sensible and can be a terrific way to put away large sums of money for future education costs. With recent changes in tax laws that eliminate federal tax on the investment earnings and make them more flexible, they may soon become the tuition savings tool of choice, but they are not perfect.

Here is how they work. The federal government granted states the power to hold and administer your college savings funds. In some states, you can contribute up to $100,000 for each child you have. Gift tax rules apply, so parents should try and keep their combined contribution to less than $20,000 in any given year. That shouldn't be too hard should it?

Under the new tax laws, the earnings on your savings in these plans are federal and in many cases state tax free forever. In certain states, you may also get a state tax deduction for the amount you contribute. Of course, if you don't happen to use the money for education purposes, you will pay all the taxes due and penalties. Since these plans take the form of trust accounts, however, you avoid the negative associated with saving money in your child's name and the cash can only be used for the purposes that you specify.

So what more could you want? The money to make a contribution would be nice. Aside from that, these plans can be confusing as each state offers a different version. They can also lack flexibility and may put control over investment decisions in the hands of the state. Also, since the assets in the plan are considered your child's, they can significantly impact the child's ability to secure financial aid in the future. Just like money saved in the child's name, these plans will count against him or her in any needs-based analysis performed to determine eligibility for scholarships, grants and even certain low-interest loans. If your child ends up attending a high-priced private school that impact can be devastating.

So if you are considering a 529 plan, my advice to you is to shop around because they are not all created equal. Remember also that you do not have to set it up in the state where you live. Check out www.collegesavings.org and you will find all sorts of information about the plans offered in various states. A word of a caution, however: If you sign up for a program in one state and your child ends up going to school in another, the implications vary. Make sure that you understand exactly what happens in those circumstances. Often you will have to pay state taxes on all the accumulated earnings.

These programs have come a long way and continue to evolve. As competition increases, they will improve even more. If you decide to set one up, simply trying to figure out in which state to do so will be a complicated business. Also, remember that future changes in tax laws can be enacted that may make them less appealing.

Trusts, Scholarships, Loans, and Aid

So, you have been in the maze for a while. Are you beginning to feel bewildered? That's a pretty common feeling parents have once they get inside. But wait, there are even more walls.

There is the wall labeled "trust fund." That's the answer — establish a trust in your child's name that you control. There can be decided tax advantages; you make the investment decisions, and your child can't burn the money on something other than college. So what could possibly be wrong with this?

A lawyer is what's wrong with this. You will need to hire a lawyer to set it up, and I strongly recommend involving a lawyer in your life only when absolutely necessary. Remember, if you need a lawyer chances are that it isn't simple. If it is simple, it won't be when the lawyer is done.

Next you come upon the walls labeled "financial aid," "scholarships," and "student loans." These are the walls that most parents find themselves staring at when the have ignored all the others — that is when they discover that they don't have enough money and begin a desperate search to see if other people will give or lend them some.

I'm not about to give you any advice on finding this free money. Hopefully, you can get yourself in a position where the importance of this outlet will be minimized. By all means, when the time comes, find out what you may be entitled to and go after it. There's a Web site called www.scholarships101.com that provides some useful information, but high school guidance counselors, college financial aid offices, and local political offices are usually the best place to start.

There are also certain education tax credits and some brand new non-itemized deductions that you may be able to take for those costs that you do end up paying out of pocket. These tax benefits can minimize the pain but only slightly in most cases.

(Sorting it All Out)

You have emerged from the maze dazed and confused. There are so many options, so many things to consider. It's no wonder parents find this to be one of the most challenging and emotionally stressful financial situations that they ever face. This is true now more so than ever as those consistently high market returns we had grown so accustomed to now seem to be a thing of the past.

Before you start to panic, relax. Free your mind of all the confusing details you have read or heard about and prepare yourself for a new way of thinking about paying for the cost of college and just keep these few simple things in mind.

There Are No Guarantees

As unpleasant as it may be to think about, less than 50% of all high school graduates enroll in a four-year college. This doesn't mean that you should assume that your child will never go on for further education, but it's entirely possible that your baby could end up in a technical school, junior college, join the military, or never go on to college at all.

The fact that you have actually been reading about the topic, however, means it's more likely that you will be the type of parent who either consciously or subconsciously pushes your child toward higher education. Either way, while you certainly should not ignore the possibility of your kid going to college, don't let the probability consume you. It's a situation that may never come to be.

Time Is on Their Side

Face it; chances are that your child is going to live a lot longer than you will. So, if they do make it to Yale or Princeton, they will probably land a great job and have 40 years of making decent money to pay back the cost of their college education. You may have only a few working years left, and you have a retirement about which to be concerned.

So if your child does have to borrow some money to pay for college or if you insist that money you borrow be paid back in whole or part by your child, the world will not stop turning and you are not a horrible parent. Do what you reasonably can do to help.

Perhaps you can agree to help by making some of the loan payments until they get financially stabilized or you may even be able to help pay off the loans at some point in the future if you are on solid footing. Just because you will not cut a check today to cover the cost of college doesn't mean that you are unwilling to help in the future. Remember, too, someday your child may inherit your money and that can be used to pay off a student loan.

Kids can also get part-time jobs during college and enroll in work-study programs to help defer some of the costs. I worked full time during college, and the work experiences were invaluable, making the transition from classroom to working life much easier.

Concentrate Less on Saving for College and More on Looking at Options

This is the single most important thing I will tell you when it comes to dealing with the economics of college education. Most people place all of their emphasis on saving money for college and pretty much ignore the equally if not more important process of shopping for a college. There are many, many things that can be done to cut the cost of a college education.

For example, there is about a $14,000 per year difference between the cost of attending an average private university versus a public one, and there are many terrific public university systems that offer an exceptional education at a fraction of the price for residents of the state where they are located. Although a degree from a school like Harvard or Notre Dame may open doors for their graduates, work experience quickly becomes more important.

In addition, local public universities and even two-year community colleges can be another practical alternative for parents and students facing major financial issues. You can check into the feasibility of transferring credits from lower cost community colleges to a full four-year college after two years of study. This strategy can save you a significant amount of money, and the degree you ultimately earn shows only the name of the school that graduated you.

Shop Around

When it comes time to begin looking at colleges, remember that higher education is a commodity. You are buying a product, and just as if you are picking out a new car, you need to search for one that meets your needs, satisfies your requirements and gives you the most bang for your buck.

Sit down with your child early on in the process and honestly explain your financial situation. If you just don't have the money, tell your child they should expect to rely upon financial aid, scholarships, loans and work to pay for some of the costs. Most of all, stress how important it will be to select a university that is a good value.

There is a lot of information available to help you find college bargains. You can go to a Web site like www.usnews.com where you can access their annual college rankings. Here you will find rankings for top public and private universities and colleges graded by measures such as graduation rates, student retention, class size and reputation.

The most interesting information is the "Best Value" rankings. Here colleges and universities are ranked based upon a ratio of overall education quality to price. This type of information can be extremely helpful and can direct you and your child to those universities where you are most likely to maximize the quality of education and minimize the cost.

Use these information sources when it comes time to do your shopping. Find out first what your child really wants to do. For example, would they prefer to stay home or go away to school? Attending a local school can obviously cut the costs significantly as you can save on room and board. If your child is considering staying at or near home after graduation, it might just be a better option to attend a local college or university. Often preference is given to graduates of local schools by local companies, rather than to graduates of nationally known universities.

Make decisions that are mutually acceptable to everyone involved and remember that compromises may be necessary because of financial constraints. If your child seems unwilling to accept that, make it clear that you will do what you can but do not intend to bankrupt yourself to pay tuition. That isn't fair to you, your family or your child.

(The College Savings Strategy)

Provided that you still have some time before your child will attend college, the simplest thing you can do is focus on a single savings strategy. Before the recent changes in tax laws, I would have suggested that you avoid the trust, the EIRAs, the tuition savings programs or separate accounts for your child and simply save in your own name. That is, turn all your attention and efforts toward saving your own money, not specifically for college but for the future security of you and your family.

That still is not a bad idea, but even a guy obsessed with simplicity cannot ignore the potential benefits associated with a not-so-simple strategy like the 529 college savings plans. If you can afford it, they are certainly worthy of consideration.

Saving in your own name, however, remains a good strategy for those who really want to keep it simple. If you are worried about giving up those lucrative tax benefits, you can earmark some long-term investments that produce little current income, like Diamonds or index mutual funds that you read about in the last principle.

Cash them in when the time comes to pay for college at what is hopefully significantly increased values and pay tax at the lower capital gains rate. Even better, you can give these appreciated investments to your child (subject to gift tax rules of course) and let them cash them out. You may pay an even lower capital gains rate.

Most importantly, avoid becoming obsessed with education savings, like so many parents are. Remember that many things can happen along the way. If you do decide to pursue an investment strategy, keep it to just one. An EIRA here, a 529 plan there, and before you know it, you have a big complicated puzzle on your hands that you may never sort out completely. Just keep it simple.

If you just can't seem to save any money for college or have reached the point where it seems virtually certain that you will not have enough, don't turn your financial life upside down in search of a solution that may not exist. Remember, a college education is first and foremost a child's investment in his or her own future and not necessarily something that must or should be handed over by a parent.

(Golden Choice)

I made the decision to attend Canisius College, a highly regarded local private school, rather than a far less expensive state university that was literally in our backyard. My parents did not necessarily agree or have the money available to pay added costs, but they respected my decision and let me do what I wanted to do.

The agreement we struck was that they would pay the equivalent cost of the state education. I went to the school I wanted and picked up the tab for the difference in cost. Through a combination of what I earned from several part-time jobs, savings and limited scholarship money, I was able to cover the costs without ever taking a loan.

It all worked out just fine as I received an excellent education and landed a great job. I truly believe that being held responsible for part of my education was a big part of the reason for my success. It was not just a place where my parents were sending me but a place where I wanted to be and was paying to go. I made the most of it.

(The Lucky Ones)

Helping your child get through college is one of the most important things you will ever do. Just as attending college should not be considered a right, paying for college should not be considered your obligation. They are both privileges.

If you are lucky enough to have a child who goes on to higher education, consider yourself fortunate. If you are able to help pay for it, consider yourself even more fortunate. If not, evaluate the alternatives and focus your efforts on finding innovative and acceptable solutions that are within your means and satisfy your child's desires.

Principle 18

Take the Anxiety out of Retirement Planning

When it comes to matters of personal finance, there is probably nothing that strikes more fear in the heart of the average working person than planning for retirement. It's really quite a difficult subject to even think about, let alone to plan for in advance. Most people have a hard time figuring out what they are going to do this weekend let alone 10, 20, 30 or even more years from now.

Many of us don't like to think about retirement in any context. Sure, we dream about the day when we can throw away the alarm clock and spend lazy days sitting on the front porch sipping lemonade and watching the sunset. Retirement, however, can also bring the challenges of advancing age in a society obsessed with youth, deteriorating health, potential loss of productivity, and loneliness. For many, even thinking about retirement seems like they have reached the end and accepted the inevitable.

(Practical Reality)

People also fail to plan for retirement for far more practical and far less psychological reasons. They simply don't have time. We are all so busy in our everyday lives with the responsibilities of work and family that retirement is about the farthest thing from our minds.

Even those people who do have the time to think about retirement planning may refuse to do so because they really don't want to know how bad off they are. They have a hard enough time just paying the monthly bills and just assume that whatever they can do for retirement is probably too little, too late.

Is savings for retirement a good idea? Sure, retirement savings is something that should be near the front of everyone's list of worthwhile things to do. Think about it, retiring without any money is really not going to be much fun at all. Surely there are more important things to have in retirement, like good health and the love of a companion, but face it—without money, retirement can be a pretty awful condition.

(Enough Is Enough)

I consider myself to be a "moderate" when it comes to retirement savings. I put money away each paycheck in my 401(k), but that's about the extent of it. All that cash has been 100% invested in the stock market since I began contributing, which until recently seemed to be a pretty sound investment strategy.

Even before the disappearance of some of my nest egg, I would be the first to admit that I have no idea whether or not there will ever be enough. My philosophy is that there are so many options, unforeseeable future events, and uncertainties that it makes little sense to go crazy worrying about it. It's clearly a case of paralysis by analysis.

Before I decided to convince others of the merits of my unconventional approach to this most difficult financial problem, I thought it would be a good idea to give formal retirement planning a try. So I went to the Internet, where you can find Web sites like www.smartmoney.com and www.vangaurd.com.

(Number Crunching)

I accessed a neat little piece of software that allowed me to prepare a comprehensive retirement plan. After entering some personal information, I was asked for details about our income, expenses, assets, liabilities, and even rates of return on our investments. You can provide this data at a very high level or at varying levels of painstaking detail.

What the software ultimately does is calculate how much money you will have left on the day your retirement ends, in other words, up to your death. Where you don't give specific information, assumptions are made. In the name of research, I provided as much detail as possible.

After a couple of hours of input I was ready to find out the results. I had done all the work, adding up monthly bills, built in reasonable assumptions about housing costs, projected investment income, provided details about my 401(k) and retirement plan, and even went back to our tax return to figure out a tax rate. It was a complete, comprehensive analysis and admittedly not all that difficult to do.

I must admit to a sense of dread in my stomach just before I made that final mouse click. It felt as if I was about to get the results of a final exam. The time had come to find out how bad off we really were. I clicked and waited. We are projected to have $12,749,417 or $1,292,538 in inflation adjusted dollars left over at the end of our retirement at age 90! This retirement planning isn't such a bad thing after all. If I had known what the results were going to be, I would have done it years ago.

The pessimist in me quickly decided that the result was just too good, so I went back through the details and made sure that I had entered everything correctly. It seemed that all the revenue, expense, and investment information that I had entered was accurate. What could be wrong? Finally it hit me like a cold wind. After entering all of my current income and expenses, the software concluded that I had thousands of dollars left over each month to invest.

Now if I compare our fixed monthly expenditures to our combined take-home pay, the math would show that we have at least $1,500 left over each month. As such, the software figured that we should be saving $18,000 a year. It seems that unless you tell it otherwise, the difference between what you make and what you your expenses are, gets plugged into your investment balance by default—perfectly logical, I might add.

(Disappearing Dollars)

The sobering reality was about to set in on me. After 15-plus years of marriage, how much had we actually been able to save? I can tell you it wasn't anything close to $18,000 a year. Like it or not, we spend a heck of a lot more money each month than the total of all those fixed expenditures that I had input.

I decided to recalculate. This time, however, rather than go through all the details, I simply input a total annual expense amount, calculated by taking our after-tax income and subtracting the amount of money we were able to save last year. The difference, whether or not we can identify it, represents our real annual "expenses."

The result was not nearly so encouraging. Our savings will be completely gone in the year 2031, which is 20 years too early. My worst nightmare had come true.

(Questionable Results)

This experiment convinced me of something I believed to be true all along. Retirement planning is basically an exercise in futility! Now I am not suggesting that you stick your head in the sand and ignore it completely. But just provide incorrect or unreasonable information as I did, and you can end up with dramatically different results. With just a few keystrokes, I went from an ocean front condo in Hilton Head to a trailer park in Toledo.

What really makes me question the value of traditional retirement planning is the incredible number of assumptions that must be made, assumptions that are so key to the analysis but that involve future events over which you have virtually no control. For example:

Pension Benefits

Your pension is a key variable in the retirement calculation, and there are many unpredictable factors that can significantly impact this, especially if you are years away from collecting one. Your company may not be around when you retire. You may change or lose you job, forfeiting some or all of the benefits on which you were counting. In this day and age of rapid technological change and business consolidation, can anyone who is not near retirement age really count on collecting a pension from his or her current employer?

Many people, especially younger workers, are not even aware of how their pension works. In the old days of so-called "defined benefit" plans, if you worked for a company for a certain number of years you were assured of a certain payment amount each month. With "defined contribution" plans that are so popular today, however, your employer contributes a predetermined amount that gets invested. Whatever is there when you retire belongs to you, and your benefit payments are determined accordingly. That is, your pension depends upon how well your investments did. Many employers do not even allow you to select those investments. They do it for you.

Although it's difficult to predict how much you can count on from any plan, I urge you to go to your human resources office and get all the specific details of how your pension works, including details regarding health insurance and prescription drug coverage. Remember that if you leave a job even after a short stay, you may be entitled to some benefits down the road. Find out what they are, get it in writing, and put it safely away in your "Job" file. But don't try to project that out 20 or 30 years!

Social Security

Another big variable in the retirement planning equation is Social Security. I would guess that somehow the Social Security system will survive, but who knows. What's going to happen over the next 25 years? Your guess as is good as anyone's. So do we keep the Social Security income in the analysis?

Spending Habits

This is one of the most difficult elements of the analysis to predict. Can you realistically assess how much money you will be spending 5, 10, 15, even 30 years from now? There are so many variables to consider. You could have more or fewer kids than you planned, you might end up paying for the care of an elderly parent, financing large unplanned medical bills, moving into a bigger or smaller house, or buying a boat or a vacation home. On top of that, you have no idea how long you are going to live.

Income

Will you stay at your current job or get a new one paying twice or half as much? Your spouse might decide to quit his or her job and stay home with the kids. You could start your own business. Who knows?

Investments

All sorts of unpredictable variables can influence projected investment returns. The stock market could realize dramatic returns in either direction. You could pick the "right" or the "wrong" investment strategies, hit it big or lose your shirt on an individual stock. How much will be in our 401(k) and IRAs? No one knows.

Life Events

You could be divorced, remarried or start a second family. You may collect life insurance proceeds, win the lottery or inherit some money. Be careful if you plan on factoring an inheritance into your retirement equations. Unless it's safely away in a trust, inheritances have a way of disappearing, especially if the person leaving it to you happens to need long-term care.

(Plan for Uncertainty)

Corporations hire teams of talented finance people to put together annual operating plans and budgets. These plans generally include sophisticated projections of future revenue and expenses based upon exhaustive analysis of historical data using complex modeling techniques.

Most often these detailed plans cover a one-year period with more broad-based assumption going into plans that stretch out two or maybe as long as five years. Few corporations attempt to plan out beyond five years with any level of detail. There are just too many variables that can change.

The facts are that hardly any of these plans ever hit it on the head. So, if the scores of experts working months on plans are consistently wrong, sometimes even way out of the ballpark, how can you expect to do better? In addition, the variables that can impact our plans are far greater in number and far more unpredictable.

Unlike a corporation, you and I also have the added burden of human emotion. There are events that will occur over the years that will dramatically shape your financial profile, decisions that are driven not by bottom-line analysis but by thoughts and feeling, making the future even more difficult to predict. Unless you are close enough to the point where retirement is virtually upon you and many of those variables have become clear and major decisions made, it is virtually impossible to foresee the future with any level of accuracy.

So is retirement planning a game that should not be played because it's impossible to win or even get inside the ballpark? Maybe, but regardless of the seemingly infinite number of variables that can impact the outcome, some limited planning for retirement can pay big dividends in the future.

(Golden Rules for Golden Years)

If you are concerned that your best meal of the week during your golden years will be 49-cent cheeseburger night at the local burger place, and you insist on doing some formal retirement planning, here are a few simple things to keep in mind:

Traditional Retirement Planning Is Experimental Science

Don't get too caught up in traditional retirement planning. Most models and plans are far more detailed than most people need and contain too many variables for you to stand even a reasonable chance at trying to predict accurately. They are mostly the inventions of brokers, financial planners and insurance companies who are interested in shocking you into buying products.

Bad Data Equals Bad Results

If you use a retirement planning model, don't get too worried or too confident in the results. Remember, inaccurate predictions or bad information about seemingly insignificant variables can dramatically alter the results. I went from being a multimillionaire to running out of money in just a few keystrokes.

You May Not Need as Much as You Think

Most people who formally plan for their retirement do so during the period of their lives when their spending is at its peak. It's only natural to assume that spending patterns will carry over into the retirement years. Although true for some, the vast majority of folks will realize dramatic decreases in their spending during the years immediately preceding and during retirement.

(Mom and Dad)

I use my own parents as an example of what I am trying to say. We never had a lot of money growing up, but we were always comfortable, well provided for and had our share of fun.

I know it wasn't always easy for my parents to get by over the years. I'm sure retirement planning was the farthest thing from their minds. Dad retired several years ago and both he and Mom now collect a reasonable pension from his years of working on the railroad. When he called it quits, they had a modest sum of money tucked away. It was nothing dramatic, just a nice little nest egg. Their house has long been paid off, and they have not had a car payment, credit card or any other form of debt for as long as I can remember.

The kids were gone from home and college bills had long been paid in full. They owed nothing to anyone. They had all the material possessions they could ever want and then some.

My Dad is an avid train collector with an impressive collection. He spends his days puttering around the house, taking day trips to train shows and roaming the malls. They traveled a bit at first, spending a month in Florida each January to escape the heart of winter. Mom is now content staying home, relaxing with a good book or watching television. They run errands around town, go out to dinner a couple of nights a week, and enjoy the company of each other, good friends, their children, and grandchildren.

Now some 15 years after retirement, from all observations, it's been a wonderful success, and they have done it without the benefit of a huge amount of money saved up front. There is absolutely nothing they want. In addition, they drive nice cars, own a comfortable home and can go out and buy anything they need.

In fact, every year they complain when it comes time to withdraw money from their IRAs. You see, they just don't need it! The pension check more than covers their monthly expenses and even finances the more than occasional model toy train purchase. I often wonder if Mom and Dad had done one of those retirement planning models 30 years ago what it would have told them they needed to save. I cannot imagine what they would have done if they had a big 401(k) payout waiting for them, as they can't spend what they have now.

Granted they are among the lucky ones, having been fulfilled in their retirement years, and financially secure living a modest lifestyle thanks to decent health insurance, Social Security, a good pension and their savings. I'm not suggesting that everyone will end up as well off as my parents. Think about it though, you may have a better shot at it than you think, even if you don't do any retirement planning at all. Perhaps I have been too optimistic when it comes to my attitude. Many financial planners would shudder at my all too rosy outlook.

(What the Future Holds)

We all dream of a glorious retirement, filled with sunshine, laughter and timeless days spent enjoying the fruits of our la- bors and just watching the world go by and relaxing. Perhaps your dreams include a beautiful retirement home, a new luxury car, a boat or traveling the world.

For some people, retirement lives up to these expectations. For others, retirement will become a far less glamorous proposition. What seems appealing to you at age 40 or 50 may not seem quite the same at age 70. Chances are that you will settle close to the ones you love. Rather than spending a day walking on a Caribbean beach, you may prefer spending it teaching your grandchild how to fish or plant flowers. A luxury car may be less appealing than a comfortable recliner.

This is not to suggest that everyone should expect to live a life of mediocrity in retirement. Expect it to be wonderful, just be reasonable with your expectations. Don't waste the prime years of your life obsessing over events that may never take place and agonizing about saving money that you may never need.

Don't be scared by financial planners trying to rope you into unbearable savings plans, commission-rich annuities, or "investment grade" life insurance that pays them most of the first year's premiums as fees.

Far too many people get petrified and live lives filled with anxiety worrying about events that will not occur. It's reasonable to have some concerns about providing for your retirement. I am not suggesting that you give no thought to the future.

Here are a few more important and simple things you can do and should consider when it comes to planning for your retirement:

Don't Rule Out Continuing to Work

Believe it or not, many people find that retirement is not all they thought it would be, so they end up returning to work. There are more job opportunities for seniors now than at any time in the past as employers realize that responsible seniors can make far better employees than energetic teenagers.

That doesn't mean you will have to serve up burgers and fries either. There are plenty of meaningful and fun positions available for retired people. Perhaps you will take a part-time job as a starter at the local golf course, a sales consultant at a bridal boutique, arranging flowers, or selling real estate.

There are also countless at-home business ventures. Many of these jobs can provide you with decent supplemental income and benefit opportunities, including health insurance that in and of itself can make it worth your while.

Give to Your 401(k) Until It Hurts

If you do nothing else in preparation for your retirement, contribute as much as you can possibly afford to your 401(k). Most of us know about 401(k)s. They are self-directed retirement funds sponsored by your employer where you can put a percentage of your earnings away on a pre-tax basis.

Many employers also offer matching provisions. That is, they put in an additional amount for each amount you contribute. You are taxed as you withdraw the funds in retirement. It's difficult to get money out of your 401(k) early without incurring a substantial penalty, which actually makes them an even more attractive savings option. You can find plenty of good information about 401(k) plans at Web sites like www.401k.com.

(The IRA)

If you don't have a 401(k), put money into an IRA. Like everything that has to do with the Internal Revenue Service, the rules can be complicated. Basically, any working person can currently contribute to an IRA. If you are not covered by a retirement plan or even if you are and make less than a specified amount, your contribution will be tax deductible. You can even contribute on behalf of a non-working spouse.

The earnings on your investment are not taxed until you withdraw the money beginning at age 59 ½, even if you could not claim a deduction for your contribution. At 70 ½, you must start pulling out the money. Like your 401(k), getting money out of your IRA before you reach retirement age will cost you.

You might also consider a Roth IRA. Although no one gets a tax deduction for the contributions, withdrawals are tax free if you are over age 59 ½. That's right, you pay no tax ever on the earnings. If you pull the money out early you will pay the taxes and a substantial penalty, unless the money is used to do something like buy your first house.

IRAs can be set up at your local bank and at mutual fund companies and are offered in a wide range of instruments and accounts. Try to keep them as consolidated as possible. Once you set them up, 401(k)s and IRAs can be a painless way to save for retirement.

(Building a Nest Egg)

The money in these accounts is virtually untouchable without incurring significant penalties, which should make you think twice before spending it on something other than retirement.

In addition, as we discussed earlier, 401(k)s can provide you with an extremely valuable source of savings, not only for retirement but also savings for life's other big events, as you can access your accumulated balances by borrowing from yourself.

You can do some pretty magical things with 401(k)s, especially when your employer throws in a matching contribution. They are relatively painless, but if history repeats itself, you can quickly build some impressive balances.

If your retirement is beyond 10 years out, consider directing everything into a stock-based investment. Pay no attention to interim price movements. Play the averages and be confident that over a long period of time your small weekly savings is helping to build a solid retirement future.

(Take Care of the Present)

After all this, you are probably still wondering what to do about retirement planning. The simple answer to this very complex question is "change your focus." The future is filled to capacity with uncertainty. That's part of the challenge. Get your current financial life in order so things fall into place naturally as you near retirement. Rather than agonizing over all the variables in a traditional retirement plan that you have little or no control over, try focusing on the things you can control.

A traditional retirement plan might tell you that you need to save $4 million by age 65 and to get there you must start putting away $600 per month in investments that yield at least 8%. Meeting the savings objectives of these traditional plans is virtually impossible for most of us. The numbers are so astronomical that it can be psychologically damaging to even know what they are.

Rather than subjecting yourself to such agony, simply concentrate on the factors that can influence your retirement rather than on a retirement plan. For example, find out all the specifics about your company retirement plan.

The Social Security Administration now automatically sends working people personalized projections of expected monthly benefits. Look it over and keep it.

Contribute as much as possible to your 401(k) or IRAs but don't get too frustrated or depressed if that's all you manage to do. Instead, concentrate on things like getting your home equity loan paid off and your credit cards under control.

Work on that side business that you always wanted to start. Buy your retirement home and start paying for it. Make job decisions that will help to ensure that you will receive a pension and paid health insurance. Do not focus so much on maximizing retirement savings but rather on improving your retirement condition. Putting $100 a week away toward a $4 million goal will hardly keep you motivated. Instead, get your financial house in order by working to ensure that your expenses will be low and your cash flow high.

This approach will grate on some people, who may read it as a "why worry" approach. Please, don't take it that way. The problem is that for far too many people, the retirement planning process has become a nightmare. My approach is to adopt a common-sense, realistic approach. Anyway, getting worked up about something that you cannot change will not help.

Do what you can to make things as financially sound as possible during your working years but don't take all the enjoyment out of your life by obsessing over retirement. Be cognizant of your retirement needs, make decisions that will help to secure your future, and stop all the endless analysis of unpredictable events. Remember, retirement is as much about the present as it is about the future, and with a little common sense and good luck, the future will take care of itself.

Principle 19

Buy Peace of Mind with Insurance

You are relaxing in your favorite coffeehouse when an interesting looking gentleman approaches you. "What are you drinking?" he asks in a calm and sophisticated manner. "Cappuccino," you respond. "Come here often?" he queries. "Every day on my way to work," you respond. "How old are you?" Thinking that it is really none of his business you respond that you are 40. "Have a family?" Beginning to wonder if you should continue this conversation you respond cautiously, "Yes, I have one child."

He sits down beside you. "Look sir, if you are trying to sell me something I'm really not interested, and if you are just trying to be friendly, it's not working too well." Curiously, he looks at you and responds, "I'm sorry if I make you uncomfortable, but I was just wondering if you could answer one more question for me?" Assuming he is not about to go away and feeling a bit embarrassed by how polite he is being, you respond, "Sure, what is it?"

Just finishing a long, slow sip from his caffé mocha he proceeds, "Well I was just wondering, for the price of that cup of cappuccino you are drinking, would you consider securing the future of your family forever?" Ah ha! He is trying to sell something. What is it? You are not about to hang around and find out. Quickly you grab your cup and walk toward the door. Just before you exit, you turn for one last look at the stranger, and to your astonishment, he is gone.

Was this some sort of mystical vision or merely a close encounter with a salesperson? You may never know for sure, but one thing you should know is the answer to his question. It is possible to secure the future of your family for about the price of a cup of cappuccino a day. Is it a magic potion, a hot stock or a pyramid scheme? No, it's life insurance, and it can be one of the most important purchases you will ever make.

Life insurance is also perhaps one of the most psychologically difficult purchases that a person can ever make, for no one wants to think about ever needing it. Many people just don't believe in life insurance, preferring to spend the money on living. Actually I think life insurance sales could be boosted considerably if they simply renamed it "survivor" insurance. That's exactly who you buy it for after all.

Now think about that mystery man in the coffeehouse and about the question he asked. If for the price of a cup of cappuccino a day you could secure the future of those you love and care for, as long as they remain on this earth, would you do it? Very few of us would pass up that opportunity. If only it were that easy — well guess what, it is that easy.

(The Complexity of It All)

Life insurance can be one of the easiest financial products you will ever buy. It can also be one of the most complicated. To keep it simple, stay away from so-called *permanent insurance* and buy yourself a good *term insurance* policy. What's the difference?

Basically, permanent insurance policies, or whole life as they are also known, combine an element of savings and investment with insurance protection. That is, you pay a premium amount, which can be fixed or variable. Part of that premium gets invested and part goes to buy insurance protection that you will have until you pass away or decide to surrender the policy for cash. Term insurance is simply life insurance protection that pays your beneficiaries a fixed benefit amount when you die. You buy it for a stated period of time, and generally the premiums increase as you grow older.

If you really feel like spinning your head some day, invite a life insurance salesman over to the house and tell him or her that you are interested in a whole life policy. Before you know it, the salesperson will be talking about things like universal life, variable life, variable universal life, single premium life, and so on. He or she will tell you about the flexibility of whole life coverage, how in some cases you can control how your premiums are invested, about the dividends, the tax-free investment earnings, and the cash surrender value.

You might end up buying one, and if you do, I defy you to tell me exactly what is it you purchased and more importantly how much you are paying for the insurance protection you wanted in the first place. Don't get me wrong, whole life insurance is not necessarily a bad product; it's just not a simple product.

Insuring the future of your loved ones is not a complicated matter. The insurance policy you buy to accomplish it doesn't need to be either. If you need insurance protection, then buy insurance. If you need to invest your money, buy investments.

(Finding the Right Policy)

So you are in the market for a good term insurance policy. What is the first thing you should do? Quit smoking for one! Then go to a Web site like www.quotesmith.com.

At www.quotesmith.com, all you need to do is input some basic information, and you will be immediately provided with price quotes from a wide variety of insurance companies, as well as current AM Best ratings. AM Best is an independent company that evaluates the financial strength and stability of insurance providers. Detailed explanations of their ratings are given as well as easy links to request applications.

Many employers also provide a basic amount of life insurance at no cost and make term insurance available at very reasonable rates. Keep in mind, however, if you change jobs these policies do not generally go with you. It's better to lock in low rates from someone independent of your job for at least a portion of your coverage rather than risk trying to replace it.

(Finding the Right Dosage)

So how much term insurance do you need? That's an extremely difficult question to answer. Once again you are trying to predict a future that is filled with question marks. How many children will you have; how much money will you have saved; will your spouse continue to work; what kind of house will your family live in? These are just some of the unpredictable elements that enter into the equation.

There are two fairly simplistic and acceptable methods of estimating insurance needs that you should know about, however. Just keep in mind that they are both merely estimating techniques.

If you go to a Web site like www.smartmoney.com, you can find what is called a "financial needs based approach." That is, you can estimate the amount of money your spouse and/or kids will require over the years, then offset that against how much money you currently have saved and how much your spouse is likely to earn.

Although beneficial to give you a rough idea of insurance requirements, this is far too detailed an exercise. It gives one the impression that there is a scientific formula for determining such matters.

There is a more simplistic approach referred to as the "income methodology." You just estimate the amount of insurance you need based upon the amount of money that you currently make. A general rule of thumb is that the face amount of insurance should be equal to six to eight times your gross income. You will find more information on this and other methodologies at www.insurance.com.

(Round the Numbers)

There are so many variables that come into play in assessing how much insurance you may need that trying to predict it with any level of certainty is just as futile as trying to estimate how much money you will need in retirement. If you insist on making a science project out of this, the income methodology is the way to go. It's quick, easy and reasonable, but even that tends to be too much analysis.

Just remember that the single most important factor is whether or not the ones left behind will be able to fend for themselves. As such, everyone with small children must have some level of life insurance. If you have no children, it really becomes more of a personal choice.

So if you really want to keep this simple, just do a quick assessment of your situation and pick a nice round number, like $500,000. If that amount were invested in an account paying 5% interest, it would produce about $2,000 a month of pre-tax income. When coupled with Social Security benefits that children receive as survivors, amounts you may have saved or invested, and current income your spouse may generate, that amount may very well be sufficient. If not, just buy more.

I personally carry about $700,000 of term insurance on myself and less than half that amount on my wife. Would that be enough to provide for my daughter in the manner I would like? Who really knows, but it is a number with which I feel comfortable.

That really is the point. Do not agonize over trying to figure out the "right" number when you know up front that there is no "right" number. Simply make sure you buy the insurance and get what you believe is a reasonable amount.

(Price Tag)

Here's the best part of all. Just about anyone can afford to buy this essential protection. How much would you expect to pay for $500,000 of insurance? If you are 30 years old and don't smoke, it might cost you as little as $300 a year, and your premium will be guaranteed level for 20 years.

In other words, it costs you less than a cup of cappuccino a day to insure the future. Don't pass on this opportunity, especially if there are children who need your support.

Remember how I said the first thing you needed to do was quit smoking? Here's why. If you smoke, that same policy will cost you about $500 a year. Need I say more?

Term insurance costs more as you get older and eventually the coverage terminates. Although some people see this as a disadvantage, it can work out quite nicely as your need for insurance will be decreasing at the same time your premiums are increasing. If you choose, simply cut back your coverage amount or eliminate it all together. Some people, however, just decide to keep paying the higher premiums, so they can leave something behind for the grandchildren perhaps. Term insurance leaves that decision up to you.

(Protecting Credit)

On a related topic, it seems like everyone is trying to sell us credit life insurance these days. Whether it's the mortgage, car loan or even credit cards, for just a few dollars extra, an insurance company will guarantee that your debt will be paid off should you unexpectedly pass along. Is it a good idea? Sure it is in principle, but credit protection insurance is just another pricey complication we can do without.

The same thing can be accomplished with a single, cost-effective term insurance policy. So rather than spending your money on credit insurance, simply buy enough term insurance to ensure that there will be enough left over to pay off your debts.

(Wise Buy)

On your next trip to the coffee shop, before you take that first sip, think about the future of your family for a moment. Term life insurance is an easy product to buy, and it's even easier to own. All you have to do is pay the premiums and forget about it.

So before you make that decision to lay out money for that next vacation or for a backyard pool, make sure that you have already taken care of something much more important to your family. Buy them some survivor insurance.

(Other Insurance)

There is another type of simple insurance protection that everyone should consider getting. If you have any doubts, pick up your local phone book and look at who advertises on the back cover. Chances are that it's a law firm "specializing in personal injury cases." Now turn to the "lawyers" section of the same phone book. Notice all those big page and half-page ads, some in color, many with photographs. Generally the biggest and the most eye-catching ads belong to the personal injury lawyers, and they can cost thousands of dollars. So how do you think the lawyers afford it? Easy, they are taking on a lot of cases and winning often.

Suing has become one of America's favorite pastimes, and it's the lawyers who are convincing us to do it. Most of them will take on your case free of charge, only getting paid if they win and you get a settlement. People who would never before even consider getting a lawyer are eager to jump onboard the "litigation express." It's even better than the lottery. You can hit the jackpot without ever spending a single dollar, and if you win, it's tax free.

As lawyers have come to realize how much they can make off a good personal injury case, "victims" have come to realize the value of their suffering, and many courts and juries are very sympathetic.

What can you be sued for exactly? You name it and someone can file a lawsuit against you. Get in a serious car accident, and it's almost guaranteed someone will sue, even if they hit you. If your dog bites someone or a neighbor kid falls off your backyard swing set, get ready. Don't assume that friends and neighbors won't sue you either. You can even be sued if someone trips on the crack in the sidewalk in front of your house.

The lure of the payoff is just so large that it's virtually impossible for some people to resist. If you are unfortunate enough to be a victim of our litigation happy society, be prepared to invest a significant amount of both time and money defending yourself. It's a complication all of us can surely do without, but it is unfortunately more common each day.

(Never Go Out Without One)

So how can you protect yourself should your friendly neighborhood lawyer come knocking on your door? It's really quite easy to do, and it's known as personal liability coverage. You will often hear it referred to as an "umbrella policy."

An umbrella policy protects you from both lawyers and from yourself. Let me explain. Most of us have collision insurance on our cars and homeowner's insurance on our house. If you have an accident or if something happens to your house, these traditional products pick up the tab to have them fixed, net of a deductible.

Car and homeowner's insurance policies generally provide you some level of personal injury insurance protection; $250,000 would be a common amount on your auto policy. If someone is injured in a car accident or at your home, this insurance protects you by paying medical costs and damage awards. Once the limits of your coverage are reached, you are on your own. If the court awards a settlement amount in excess of your coverage, you pay the difference.

If you get sued for just about any reason and a settlement is awarded, your umbrella policy will kick in to cover the difference between the settlement and the liability limits on your primary auto, homeowner's or boat policy. Best of all, since it's personal insurance, it goes with you and your family no matter where you are and what you are doing.

Should someone get injured from virtually any cause other than gross negligence or criminal activity, you are protected. It also can protect you from lawsuits brought for nonphysical forms of injury such as slander and defamation of character. Make sure you check your policy for specific coverage.

(Enough Is Enough)

Sound like a good idea? It is, but figuring out how much you need is even less of an exact science than trying to estimate how much term insurance you need. As you know, I don't like to perform a lot of detailed analysis about unpredictable events. Given my fondness for big round numbers, why not keep it simple and go for $1,000,000 in umbrella coverage. Settlements that large are common today.

How much would that cost? Here's the best part. If you already have insurance coverage on your home, car, or boat with reasonable liability limits and unless you have a dangerous job or hobby, personal umbrella policies are dirt cheap. You can expect to pay about $150 a year for that $1,000,000 of protection. That's right, per year. In my opinion, aside from term life insurance there is no better value for the buck or smarter idea than umbrella insurance. You can't buy a million of anything for $150, can you?

(Relax, You're Covered)

For such a small amount of money you can relax knowing that you have protected yourself against potential ravages of someone looking to make a quick buck off an unfortunate situation. Accidents do happen, and there are legitimate and fictitious injury cases brought against people all the time.

Even more important then the "payoff" protection is the comfort that the insurance company, with its legion of attorneys, will be standing in front of you, protecting both your interests and their own. Simple protection against complex events is always a good idea.

Principle 20
Don't Put off Planning Your Estate

As a general rule, I try to avoid having a lawyer get involved in my financial affairs. Lawyers thrive on complexity. In fact, they get paid based upon how much of it they create, and most of them do an exceptional job at it.

That being said, if there were one thing I would want less involved in my personal affairs than a lawyer, it would be the government. When it comes to preparing for your ultimate demise, you better get to your lawyer. For if you don't, chances are pretty good that the government will step in and make a lot of important decisions with which you might have disagreed. So do yourself and your loved ones a big favor, get to a lawyer and prepare a will. Tell the rest of the world in no uncertain terms what you want done.

Life is an unpredictable proposition at best. Since none of us knows when the end will come, it goes without saying that none of us has any idea how long we have to take care of this most important matter. Don't delay; if you do, your family and friends may be the unfortunate beneficiaries of some unnecessary complexity.

(Final Business)

It may seem a bit cold, but let's deal with your day of reckoning from a purely financial perspective. That is, think of it in the same terms as the other major financial events you must prepare for, like college, retirement or buying a house. Take care of it once and for all and then get on with the business of living. There are many, many good reasons why it is important for you to have a will. For one thing, a will specifies who will receive your possessions. Whether it's cash, stocks, bonds, your house, car, furniture, or your computer, without a will, a court may very well end up deciding who gets what.

A common misconception is that wills are just for people with a lot of money. Nothing could be further from the truth. No matter what your financial condition, it's important to have a will. If you have a child, it's not just important, it's essential. For without a will, the decision as to who takes custody of minor children is left up to the state, and they may end up making a decision that you would not consider in the best interest of your child or other family members.

Another common misconception is that a will is a very rigid legal document. Although it's true that most wills follow a common format and contain standardized language and certain key elements, it is by no means a rigid document. You can put just about anything you want into a will and many people do just that.

You can make specific arrangements for the care of your poodle, dictate who gets your trading card collection, make sure a favorite nephew gets your car or specify that someone gets nothing. A will is your last opportunity to send a message to everyone left behind.

(Child Matters)

Most important of all, your will is the document where you specify the "guardian" who is to care for your minor children. If the other natural parent is still alive, the decision is often pretty automatic unless that parent is unable or unwilling to provide adequate care. If there is no natural parent to care for the child, however, the implications of not specifying a guardian can be significant, and the impact can be devastating on those left behind.

The best that you could hope for is that the guardian will be apparent to the court, for example: a grandparent, brother, sister, aunt or uncle. Don't count on it, however, as few things are seldom obvious in the court of law.

There may end up being an ugly custody battle if more than one person decides that he or she is the logical choice. Such battles can be long, costly, divisive and emotionally damaging to everyone involved, most notably the child.

In the worst case scenario, there may be no one apparent to the court as the logical guardian. Perhaps the grandparents are too old, and other relatives are unwilling or unable to take on the responsibility. Choices for guardians that may seem logical to you, such as good friends or more distant relatives, may not be logical choices for the court. If the court cannot find a suitable guardian, they will appoint one, and in the most tragic cases, that could be a foster parent who is a complete stranger.

Do yourself and your family a favor. Make this decision soon. If you are married, sit down with your spouse and discuss it. Who do you want to raise your child in the event that both parents are not here to do so? Do not take this decision lightly.

Talk with the people you have in mind to determine their willingness and their ability to take on the responsibility. This is no time for shyness. Don't be afraid to ask tough questions about religious beliefs, morality and personal finances before you decide.

Most good friends or close relatives will have no problem answering such tough questions when they know why you are asking. Once you decide upon a willing and able guardian, write it in your will. Name back-ups in case you first choice is unable or becomes unwilling to perform the duties.

(Money Matters)

Not only will custody of your child become an important issue, so will custody of the assets necessary to raise the child in the manner that you desire. In your will, spell out exactly who gets what and how they are to invest and spend it.

Don't make the common mistake of assuming that you have no need for a will since there will be little or nothing to manage when you are gone. Life insurance proceeds alone can be a significant amount of money. When coupled with the liquidation of your assets, including the house, car, collectibles, savings and retirement accounts, pension and Social Security benefits, etc., there may be a lot more money left over than you think.

Keep in mind that it's not necessary to give custody of the assets to the same person who has custody of the child. The choice of guardian is often a slam-dunk for many folks. Unfortunately, the person they would trust with raising the kid may be the last person they want to give the monetary assets to, as the potential guardian may not have the knowledge or ability to deal with significant sums of money. In your will, you can specify who watches over the money as well as who watches over the kids, and they don't have to be the same people.

(Tough Questions)

If you specify in your will who gets control of the assets to care for minor children, that person, known as the "custodian," will be periodically responsible for reporting back to the court as to how those assets are being invested and spent. There is no guarantee that your wishes will be carried out, however. You must select someone you absolutely trust who is on solid financial ground, and even that's no guarantee.

In addition, make sure that they have the same basic philosophies as you have when it comes to money and children. For example, ask them: what they consider to be a reasonable allowance for a child; if they would permit a class trip to Washington, D.C. or spring break in Panama City with friends; at what age they would let a child have a car; and what types of schools they prefer. Ask them anything that's important to you, and if you don't care for their answers, either pick someone else or make certain that they understand what you would do and that you can trust them to follow your wishes.

(In Trust)

If you just can't get comfortable with any one person or if you are concerned that your child will not be able to adequately handle the responsibilities of money once they reach the age of majority, an alternative would be to consider establishing a trust. Most people think that trusts are extremely complicated and only for rich people.

Truth is, anyone can establish a trust to hold assets on behalf of someone else regardless of how much those assets amount to or what they are. There are a couple of ways you can go. In either case, get as specific as you want outlining how and where the assets are to be invested. You may specify when money can be withdrawn, for what purposes, and the date when the child takes control of the assets. A trust can be a particularly useful tool to protect your assets if you have small children or children who are currently acting in a irresponsible manner.

One type of trust about which there has been much talk over the last several years is called a "living trust." Basically, you establish and turn assets over to it while you are still alive. There can be several advantages to living trusts, including tax benefits and the possibility of avoiding the sometimes lengthy legal process known as probate.

Probate is a court supervised process of distributing all your assets other than those that pass automatically to your survivors (such as jointly held property and investments, pension benefits with named beneficiaries, and proceeds from life insurance).

Living trusts are, however, not simple to establish, and you may pay high legal and tax preparation fees to keep them going. They can be a terrific solution in some specific circumstances, but most folks simply don't need one. Before you decide, talk to your lawyer, but there is usually an easier way to accomplish the same objectives.

That option, known as a "testamentary trust," takes over when you are gone. You specify exactly what you want to happen with your assets, but nothing actually goes into effect until you are gone. These trusts are much easier to establish and require virtually no on-going maintenance. You can still call all the shots.

Get as specific as you want or leave it in general terms. If you choose, specify exactly what assets go into the trust, how they get invested, managed, distributed, and at what age the child gets control.

You will have to name a person or institution to act as your trustee. The trustee is legally bound to follow your directions. If you can't find a suitable individual, consider the trust department at your local bank. If that's too impersonal, name a person and the bank as co-trustees to watch over each other.

There is one thing to note about trusts at banks. Typically, the fees can be excessive. One small trust was billed $2,600 a year for legal services despite the fact that there was no activity during the year other than interest on certificates of deposit.

The options are seemingly endless, so work with your lawyer to find one that works for you and your family. Avoid trusts that significantly complicate life for the beneficiary. Come up with a plan that is simple, practical, realistic and easy to follow for all involved. Be sure that your trust has at least two co-trustees and provides for some independent oversight other than the court. It may be a good idea to specify a CPA to do this job.

(More Details)

In addition to a will, your lawyer may also recommend that you have a "power of attorney" document. This gives the person you name the right to act legally on your behalf should you be unable to do so while you are still alive. For example, the person with power of attorney can execute contracts on your behalf and sign your checks.

In addition, the lawyer may recommend a "health care proxy" or a "health care power of attorney." Whether or not you decide to have one of these will most likely depend upon your religious beliefs.

Basically, the proxy gives instructions to medical personnel about what to do in the event that they believe that you can only be sustained by artificial means. Also, be sure to specify what your feelings are about organ donations. One sentence about this could save another's life.

(Taxing Situations)

Since this is a book about simplicity I have done everything I can to avoid any discussion involving taxes. However, taxes are an unavoidable complexity in many instances, and this is one of them. I would be remiss not to at least mention them.

I will make no attempt to educate you as to the complexities of estate taxation. Let me simply tell you that should the total value of all your assets exceed a certain amount, your estate will be subject to federal and possibly state taxes. Life insurance proceeds, for example, are not subject to income tax but do count in the determination of your estate tax.

For most people, tax planning for their estate is a relatively simple process and in many cases requires little or no planning at all. In some circumstances, however, estate tax planning can be extremely beneficial. Any good estate lawyer or CPA will be well versed on the tax implications and should be able to direct you accordingly.

(Get Moving)

I know that this isn't easy to think about, much less to do. Take the time now to prepare while your thoughts and emotions are clear and stable. Find an excellent lawyer as we have, a trusted friend you can easily work with, who has years of experience and a stellar reputation. Let him or her guide you through the process, help you make difficult decisions, and get these matters taken care of. You will sleep a little better yourself and make life a heck of a lot easier for those left behind.

Principle 21

Know What to Do If Facing Unemployment

It began just like any other Friday morning, except for the fact that by 9:00 AM small groups of co-workers could be seen anxiously gathering around their cubicles, whispering quietly to each other, speculating on whose name would be called next. By 10:00 AM, the phones began to ring.

It felt as if we were all the victims of some tragic mishap at sea. Clutching a piece of wreckage, dangling helplessly in the icy cold waters of an angry ocean, we all waited nervously, desperately hoping not to feel the violent tug of a vicious great white at our legs. One by one, however, our friends were disappearing, sucked into the depths below, consumed by a force that was far greater than our ability to resist.

Is this a scene from a Hollywood movie? Not quite, this surreal drama was unfolding right in a downtown office tower.

(Cutting Out the Fat)

It was the early 90s, and corporate America was paying the price for the decadent excesses of the 80s. Having made far too many bad decisions and far too few good ones, it was time to clean house, or "tighten the belt" as they said.

It starts innocently enough with the dreaded expense control measures. Little things begin to disappear, like free parking and the annual holiday party. Before you know it, you are paying more for health insurance, the exercise room is shut down, and the discount at the company store goes away. Soon the bigger cuts start to take hold, the ones that really hurt. First it's a hiring freeze. There's no less work, just fewer people to do it all. Next the bonuses go away, followed by a salary freeze.

It was cruel and unusual punishment, not only for those who received the dreaded Friday morning call but also for those "fortunate" enough to be left behind. Generally, the victims would be gone for about 10 minutes, but as soon as they left their desk, word spread quickly. What followed next was downright humiliating.

Trusted employees who arrived at the office that morning to put in another day of honest work found themselves being escorted by security back to their cubicle to pack up a few personal items before being shown the door. That was just a precaution to make sure they didn't cause any disturbance before the final exit.

Stunned friends and co-workers stood helplessly by, unable to find words suitable for the moment, shocked as their fellow employees and friends went through seemingly lifeless motions of packing up their desk. Without a word, they would vanish, erased from the organizational chart, a life forever changed, a few dollars saved.

(Beware the Corporate Scarecrow)

Make no mistake, corporate America has no heart, and unlike the scarecrow in the Wizard of Oz, it will never find one. It doesn't matter who you are, what company you work for, what position you hold, how long you have been there, or how important you may think you are. The cold, hard fact is that you are 100% expendable at the drop of a hat. Believe me, gone are the days when your loyalty to your employer was reciprocated.

Oh, they have nice, generic terms to describe these staff reductions, like "involuntary terminations," "reductions in force," and "cost saving personnel moves," but for the recipient of a pink slip it's all the same, and it's just plain devastating.

Although most disturbing and disruptive when it occurs in difficult economic periods, don't fool yourself into thinking that that's the only time it can happen. Mergers can do it, so can new managers who don't exactly like your style. Trusting the future of your family to corporate America in good times or bad can truly be risky business.

(The Worst of Times)

We have entered into a period of economic uncertainty. We all seem a bit uneasy about the future these days. It seems that the old rules of economic order may need to be rewritten. We now know that companies and entire industries can be crushed in a mere instant, that positive returns in the stock market are not guaranteed, and that jobs, even with the most stable and profitable of companies, are not lifetime contracts.

During bad economic times, we are constantly reminded of the fragility of our economic system. We all thought only people working for dot-com start-ups were vulnerable. Not so anymore, we now know there is no immunity from economic distress. Everyone is vulnerable.

(Battening Down the Hatches)

So, if you think you may ever need to sail in rough economic waters, make certain that there are no holes in the hull of your ship before you ever leave the port. The problem is that most people never start looking for those holes until the waters have begun to churn.

Losing a job is a psychologically damaging event. There are thoughts of inadequacy followed by feelings of helplessness, uncertainty and despair. Frustration sets in at the prospect of trying to find a new job.

The degree to which you experience negativity and devastation associated with such difficult times is directly related to how seaworthy you managed to make your personal financial vessel during good times. If your hull has been kept in good shape, free of unattended holes and your sails are strong, you will probably get through relatively unscathed. If your ship is unprepared, however, hold on tightly, find a good sturdy pail, and get ready to start bailing.

Earlier in this book I addressed what I called the spending blockbusters. These are the big items that really shape your personal financial present and future. If you fail to get these spending blockbusters under control, to patch the holes in the hull before the stormy whether sets in, economic uncertainty and a period of sustained unemployment will be at best unacceptable and at worst unbearable.

Let's face it; many of us have grown accustomed to living near the edge of financial crisis and, worse yet, have grown somewhat comfortable with it. The problem is that those living too close to the edge spend most of their time and energy trying not to fall in and devote little time to repairing or preparing their ship for stormy waters. It doesn't take long for the ship to sink when faced with the prospect of a large mortgage payment, a couple of car payments, tuition bills, hungry mouths to feed, a mountain of debt, utility bills to pay, insurance premiums, and no paycheck coming in the door.

Believe me, I have never been much of a proponent of the philosophy of sacrificing today for the sake of tomorrow when you never know what tomorrow will bring. That being said, a little reasonable preparation for tomorrow, especially in uncertain times, can go a long way toward making today and tomorrow a bit more comfortable.

(Prepare a Contingency Plan)

At work, most of us have "contingency plans" to help us get through emergency situations. Putting together a simple navigation map for plotting your course through the angry waters of a turbulent economic storm is a worthwhile investment of your time.

I'm not talking about stocking up on bottled water and buying a generator. I'm talking about a good old-fashioned, common-sense thought process going into every significant financial decision you make and some reasonable, simple preparations to try to avoid a crisis in the event that you fall victim to the economy.

In this regard, there are three key elements that you will need to address in formulating any such contingency plan. They are:

A Spending Reduction Plan

Your math skills are going to be severely tested should you unexpectedly lose your job. That math is a lot less difficult if you just do a little homework in advance.

Be prepared to take some drastic action to save your ship. That is, you must be ready to slash your expenses and you need to start thinking about it today.

Let's start with some easy targets. Individually they may seem insignificant, but these expenditures can make a big difference in your monthly cash flow during a crisis situation. The cable TV bill is a good place to begin. Forget the digital package with its deluxe movie channels. Basic cable is all you will need, if that.

Next comes the Internet. You will need it for your job search, but if you are using a high-priced ISP or cable modem, cancel it. You will just have to suffer with the annoying little pop-up ads on those bargain dial-up services or use the free service offered at the public library. Remember, too, when setting up your e-mail account, particularly the one that you put on your resume, always use something like Yahoo, so if you do have to dump your ISP you will still have an e-mail account.

Cell phones can also be a huge expense. There may be opportunities to cut those costs, especially if you are no longer under contract. You might cancel the service all together or go down to just one phone for a while.

You can have extra phone lines disconnected, stop renewing magazine subscriptions, and cancel the fancy health club memberships in favor of the local YMCA. The piano lessons and gymnastics can go on hold for a while. Cut out the tickets to sporting events and the theater.

Some costs may automatically be eliminated or reduced when you or your spouse stop working, such as lunches, parking and transportation, dry cleaning costs, and day care. If you really stop and think about it, and you should, there are many expenses that you can easily and dramatically cut during a period of unemployment.

Remember that all those little time versus money decisions take on a whole different meaning during a period of unemployment. Now you will have more time to spend dealing with the nickels and dimes of everyday living, something I normally consider a waste of valuable time.

There are bigger expenses that can also be looked at, like cars, houses, and education costs, but unfortunately, they are not always easy to address. Cutting these expenses often requires drastic measures, and although they should be considered as options in your plan, the long- and short-term implications must be carefully evaluated before you ever act upon them.

Remember, too, some costs are likely to rise, like health care. Employers must offer you extended care for a period of time, but you will have to pay for it and it's not cheap.

The most important part of all this discussion, however, is not about cutting expenses and estimating costs. It's about understanding what all these variables are well in advance of the storm. Most people start looking at ways to slash expenses after they receive the pink slip. Crisis management skills are then called to action, and let's face it; few of us are very good at managing in a crisis. Worse yet, many expenses are locked in, and it's just too late to do anything about them.

Don't let the prospect of losing your job consume you but always keep the possibility that it could happen in the back of your mind before making any material spending decision, especially when it comes to the spending blockbusters. So before you commit to that mortgage or car payment, sit down and figure out how long the ship would stay afloat if you lost some or all of your income.

Prepare a top-level analysis today estimating how much money would come in from sources such as unemployment insurance, spousal income, etc. and how far you could trim expenses in a crisis. Contact your employer's human resource department about severance policies and the state employment department about unemployment benefits in advance of needing them. Know what you are entitled to and use this information to make intelligent decisions.

Beware of contractual commitments for seemingly innocent things that lock you in to fixed expenses, like long-term service agreements for your cell phones for example. Don't be so quick to renew an expired contract just to get the latest phone. Avoid offers like those giving you cash to buy a new PC when you commit to years of Internet service. Car leases, for all that's good about them, also lock you into fixed payments that are almost impossible to get out of before the contract is up.

Think before you commit to any contractual relationship. Especially longer term ones like a mortgage. Many people like the idea of taking out a shorter term mortgage, say 15 years.

Consider a longer term, or a less expensive house in the first place. It's the cheapest debt you will probably ever have, and the rate differential after tax between short- and long-term rates is generally insignificant.

So why lock yourself into a bigger payment? Take the longer term. That lower payment will look pretty nice if no paycheck is coming in. If things are going well, just send in additional principal and pay it off over whatever period you want. Think long and hard before splurging on a vacation timeshare or a second home, particularly if you have to finance it.

Just a little, simple preparation can go a long way at alleviating the anxiety associated with uncertain economic times, and should the unfortunate happen, you will be well positioned to spend all your time doing what is really important—finding a new job.

A Job Search Plan

What is the single most important thing you can do when you lose your job? The answer, of course, is find a new one. Not an easy assignment, I admit, especially if everyone around you is also losing his or her job at the same time. That's why it's so important to start preparation for your job search well in advance of ever needing a new job. It's really very easy to do. Unfortunately, most people never even think about it until faced with the prospect of immediate unemployment.

If you begin to sense things are rapidly deteriorating around you, don't just sit idly by waiting for the ax to fall. Get moving and take immediate action. Most people already know the standard job search routine. Look in the Sunday classified ads, visit decent national and local employment Web sites, contact search firms or attend job fairs.

Many people, however, miss the most important routine: keeping in touch with old work friends and contacts. That can be the very best way to find employment; many of the traditional barriers are already avoided when you get referred into a job opportunity. It only makes good sense to keep up contact with all those people you have met in your career.

Maintain an updated contact list of people you meet at seminars, conferences, on sales calls or that work for competitors. Get their e-mail addresses and phone numbers. Note the names of employment agencies and recruiting firms that call you, even if you have no current interest in the job they are pitching.

Even if you don't sense imminent danger, you should actively prepare a strategy. Always keep an updated resume on file. Every time you change employers or positions, make sure you update it. The last thing you need to worry about when facing unemployment is creating a new one.

An Emergency Funding Plan

I know that all the experts tell you to put away six months worth of salary in preparation for an extended period of unemployment. Well, why don't you just save a year or two years of salary while you're at it, if it's that simple?

There is no question that putting away a half-year's pay is a great idea, but it's simply impractical for most people to do. They just don't have that kind of disposable income.

So, let's assume you don't have a mattress full of cash. What can you do? That big unused line of credit on your home equity loan I suggested that you get but never use will look really nice if you lose your job.

When you are unemployed, it's virtually impossible to find credit, but with that unused home equity line, you already have credit and they can't prevent you from using it. Should it become absolutely necessary, you can write yourself a few checks to get yourself through the rough spots, even pay off that 401(k) loan until you get enrolled in a new plan and can borrow again.

Of course, remember you will also get your entire 401(k) paid out to you, so you can conceivably use it to pay bills or for other purposes. Just remember, any of the amount distributed that doesn't make its way back into another 401(k) or IRA within six months of disbursement is subject to a penalty and back taxes. It's not an attractive option, but in a desperate situation it can be an option.

The unused balance on your financing credit card can also come in handy, especially if you have chosen one with a low fixed rate of interest. No one likes to do it, but if absolutely necessary, a low-rate credit card might provide the liquidity you need to get through a period of unemployment.

Again, just a little bit of thought during good times can go a long way toward making the bad times easier to handle. Remember that credit is hard to come by when you need it. So, does that mean you should accept all the credit offered to you? Absolutely not, all that complexity will make things worse in good times or bad. All you need to do is make intelligent decisions about choosing and using the few credit products you do need.

Always remember that credit is the absolute last resort. The first thing you will need to do is find a job. If that doesn't work right away, cut expenses. Only when it is **absolutely** necessary do you tap into borrowed money or spend your invested savings or retirement funds.

(Give Me a Break)

There you are, sitting in front of a stack of unpaid bills hoping for a financial miracle to occur. The expenses have been cut to the bone, the revenues are drying up, savings are exhausted, and your credit is tapped out, but the bills just keep on coming. What do you do next? Why, pick up the phone of course and start talking with the people to whom you owe money. You will be amazed to what lengths creditors will go to help you get through difficult times if you are up front and honest with them.

Contact your creditors at the first sign of trouble. Don't wait until you have spent all your savings and maxed out your credit cards. If you explain the situation, they will generally work to accommodate you with a satisfactory payment arrangement until you can find your way to calmer waters.

Avoid calling any of those personal credit services or lawyers who specialize in debt reduction and consolidation you hear about on TV. Rather, contact the individual creditors, and they will make arrangements with you directly or they will refer you to a service with which they maintain a relationship.

This is a reason to keep that puzzle as simple as possible. It will be a whole lot easier dealing with just a few creditors rather than an entire army of them. Also, try to stick with traditional banks or credit unions for your loans. Since they are in your neighborhood, they tend to be less aggressive and more accommodating during tough times. Finance companies and department stores can be ruthless in their collection efforts.

(Taking Advantage of the Opportunity)

Difficult economic times, getting laid-off and losing a job are not very pleasant things. However, as emotionally trying and stressful as these periods are in your life, it is possible to use them in order to motivate yourself to make some meaningful and long overdue improvements. There are only a handful of negative emotions that are stronger than fear and insecurity about the future.

Use this negativity to your advantage and channel it into positive action. There will be plenty of hours for you to use in other ways. You could watch reruns on TV or do something a bit more constructive, like cleaning up your financial mess. Get your files in order, inventory all the pieces to your puzzle and then start to apply the principles of simplification.

You can also use this period of uncertainty to motivate yourself into taking action to achieve more financial independence or make personal improvements. Maybe you have been thinking about starting a home-based business, going back to school, looking for a new job or even writing a book. Get back into the gym or start that diet you have been putting off for months. Now is the time.

If your period of unemployment is sustained, consider taking a part-time job or one that pays even significantly less than what you were making in your previous position. Not only will this keep you active in the workplace, potentially gathering more job leads, it will also bring in much needed cash and may offer important benefits like health insurance. Before you do this, make sure that you check out the impact it will have on your unemployment insurance or severance.

Stay alert and aware, make adequate preparations, and most of all start plotting a path immediately that will take you around the most turbulent waters. If you are unfortunate enough to get caught in the storm, or worse yet should you get a hole in your hull, stay calm. Focus on patching the hole and try as hard as you can to keep an even keel. Remember, eventually the waters are going to calm, and the sun will shine brightly again, guaranteed.

Principle 22
Make Charity Personal

It seems that there are just no safe havens for investors these days. No matter which direction you turn, volatility and uncertainty are about the only things you can be sure to find. If you are seeking relief from the anguish, you may wish to consider investing in something that will guarantee you an exceptional return with no risk of loss.

No, you won't find this in the stock market, real estate or the Las Vegas strip. You won't need a broker to buy this investment. In fact, all you really need to do is look outside your door to find this investment opportunity. You will find it in your local soup kitchen, family crisis centers, community hospitals, youth programs, churches, schools, senior centers, and counseling offices.

There are many things we can do with our money and each of us makes very personal choices in this regard. Some are out of necessity, but others are pursuant to our endless search for satisfaction and contentment. Whatever you do with your money, few things can bring you more emotional satisfaction than giving it away.

Philanthropy is generally a termed reserved for the rich and famous. I'm not exactly sure why rich people all of sudden turn philanthropic. It seems that maybe they develop a social consciousness or perhaps they are just trying to secure their position for eternity in whatever existence comes next.

(The Good, the Bad and the Unknown)

We have all heard the horror stories, legitimate and not-so-legitimate companies taking advantage of generosity by soliciting donations or selling products on behalf of charities that end up receiving only a small fraction of the proceeds. When you receive those phone calls it seems cold and insensitive to say no, but you can never be sure just how much of the proceeds from the sale of those frozen pizzas is really making its way to people in need. It's easy to become desensitized, confused and even angry to the point where you can't differentiate the real causes from the schemes whose only intention is to separate you from your dollars.

(The Emotion of Giving)

I am absolutely committed to supporting charities like the United Way, my church, organizations funding research to cure diseases, relief efforts, etc. There are literally hundreds of thousands of worthwhile causes wanting and needing our support. In fact, there are so many worthwhile charities and causes that some people decide not to support any of them or simply give a few dollars each paycheck to the United Way and let them figure it out.

There is absolutely nothing wrong in allowing large organizations that have the resources and experience to sort out the need and get the assistance where it belongs to take care of the dirty work for you. That being said, it's a fairly antiseptic way of doing things.

Every spending decision we make involves emotion at some level. Often, satisfaction is the primary result we are looking for when the decision is made to part with dollars. Going out to dinner with friends, a family vacation or buying new furniture are examples of spending decisions that rank high on the personal satisfaction index.

If only we could learn to derive as much satisfaction from giving as we do from spending, the world would certainly be a better place. If you are ever to find the true joy in giving your money away, you must make it personal.

(The Opportunities Are Everywhere)

There are so many ways to help that I really don't know where to begin. Many people get involved in supporting a charity because of something that hits close to home, like a disability, illness or experience with problems like addiction or abuse.

I am not about to make suggestions on charities you should support. What I will tell you, however, is that if you are to ever derive true satisfaction from charity, if you are to ever make a difference, you need to find something you believe in, something to which you will commit. You must find your passion, and once you do, figure out how you can help most.

Be creative with your charitable endeavors. For example, consider adopting a local hockey team that can't afford uniforms. Donate a couple of cases of baby formula to your community hospital to give out to young mothers who otherwise may not be able to afford it. Turn over the keys to your used car to a church retirement home. Buy a television set for the local youth group or children's books for a community daycare facility.

You don't have to be rich either to make a difference. Oftentimes, relatively small expenditures of money can make a huge impact to a struggling organization. Even if you can't give them your money, you can always give them your time, which is often worth more. Maybe you could deliver meals on wheels or become a foster parent or a big brother or big sister. Volunteer to coach the basketball team at the local youth center or teach adults how to read at the local library.

There are endless opportunities for you to put your time and money to work close to home. If you are a bit overwhelmed by it all, start by speaking with a local religious or community leader. They all have very long lists of people and organizations in dire need of assistance. It's up to you to decide how you can put your talents or resources to work to assist them in the best manner.

(The Art of Giving)

It is impossible to tell someone how to give away his or her money. The decision is a very personal one and must be made carefully if you are ever to find satisfaction in your efforts.

Pick something, anything you believe in, and then find the best way to help. If you prefer that it not get too personal, then go ahead and just write a check. But if that isn't enough for you, if you still need more, find it. There is absolutely nothing wrong in wanting to see or experience firsthand the impact of your charity.

Once you get the ball rolling, you will be amazed at how much good one person can really accomplish. Search for unconventional ideas that will spark your interest. Most of all just make sure that you share your good fortune with those in need. There is no investment you can make that will ever match the returns you will get by investing in others.

Principle 23

Take Little Steps to Make Big Changes

So you are feeling a little down, perhaps even a bit angry, out of control and uncertain about the future. The world has suddenly changed before your eyes. Maybe it's the decline in your 401(k) balance that has you down or perhaps it's just those perpetual credit card bills that you told yourself would be paid off years ago. Maybe you are worried about where the money is going to come from to pay for college or that you don't have enough saved for retirement.

You have been gainfully employed for years now but are struggling to get ahead. Sure, you have a house, a car, and a lot of nice things, but there is a lot of debt that goes along with it. When it comes to finances, you feel as if you have been treading water, never managing to move forward more than a few feet. Your savings and investment portfolios are not where you would like them to be, and whenever you do start to see progress, something inevitably sets you back. It's been a recurring pattern for some time now and you are wondering if you can ever break free.

Maybe your feelings are not this extreme or your situation not quite this bad. Still, you are far from where you would like to be at this point and see no way to get to where you want to be in the near future.

(The Power of Thinking Negatively)

Our financial situations are as diversified as our personalities, each uniquely different with its own set of characteristics, traits and quirks. If there is one shred of commonality that binds us all together, however, it's the fact that virtually no one is completely satisfied with where they are financially. It seems that we can never make enough money or have enough wealth.

If you have a job making $50,000 a year, you want one making $100,000 a year. If you own a 2,000 square foot home, you will look at one with 3,000 square feet. If you manage to save $20,000, you will convince yourself you need $40,000. If the return on your mutual fund was 10%, you want 20%.

It's basic human nature to always want more. The problem is that many people spend their entire lives in an endless quest for more, never content with the present and always looking at the future, comparing themselves to everyone else. Take it from a guy who has been there, it's an exercise in futility. There will always be someone with a bigger house, a faster car, a better job, or a larger bankroll. If you continually focus on what you don't have, rather than on what you do have, your attitude toward life will grow more and more negative by the day.

However, a little discontentment is not always bad. If channeled properly and not allowed to overwhelm you, feelings of dissatisfaction can help keep you driven and motivated. The challenge is to keep the proper level of discontentment so that it serves as a minor irritation and not an overwhelming annoyance that will force you to give up. Rather than fight your inadequacies, accept them and channel the negative energy into action.

Don't worry; I'm not about to feed you one of those "think happy thoughts" speeches. By all means, it is pretty difficult to convince people to do that anymore. Not that I have anything against positive thinkers, but I am so far removed from being one that the concept is lost on me. I find it impossible to simply think that things are going to work out okay; I need proof. In other words, I can only think positively when I have evidence that a positive outcome is likely.

Our personal financial situations present a great opportunity to unleash the power of negativity. To be successful, start off with the understanding that it's practically impossible to ever achieve exactly what you want. Stop focusing on the broader picture and accept the fact that you will never find financial nirvana.

Once you do that, begin focusing on the little things. Then take small steps to start correcting them. Build a base of positive historical experiences. It may not be possible to reach your ideal, but it's not impossible to change things in a positive direction. Do so by setting a series of short-term, achievable objectives and allowing yourself to actually reach them.

(Facing the Future)

Most people lack a sense of confidence and security in their personal financial situation. Every day, they experience that uneasy feeling that financial crisis is always looming just outside their doorstep. The loss of a job, a prolonged disability or illness, even a large unplanned expenditure could push them over the edge. They never seem to be able to enter a comfort zone when it comes to personal finances. The search to find it is even more difficult today.

It is not a pleasant thing when you have to face every day without a sense of security. It's human nature to want to feel protected and safe from harm, to be independent and self-sufficient. When you are uncomfortable with your finances, you often feel none of these things.

We all make choices throughout our lives about things like education, career, spending, savings, investing, or protecting our future that influence the level of financial security that we eventually achieve. There are also circumstances out of our control that can unwittingly push us farther and farther away.

People who live for an extended period of time without a sense of security in the future eventually turn negative. Money is to blame for all of their problems. It's common to hear phrases like "my job doesn't pay me enough," "my mortgage payment is too high," "day care costs me a fortune," or "after I pay the bills I have practically nothing left." If you live without financial confidence for too long, you might just stop fighting all together and adopt the attitude that you will "never get ahead."

(You Made the Mess So Clean It Up)

If you are facing perpetual financial uncertainty, every effort must be made to find more fertile grounds. Even those who are moderately confident but still feel that the financial security they so desperately seek has and forever will elude them must take action to improve.

This will not happen without a fundamental change in attitude. Simply refuse to accept that you will always be just one lost job or a significant unanticipated expenditure away from falling over the edge. Rather, channel your fear of the future into positive action.

Is this easier said than done? Of course, it is far easier said than done. The first step, however, is to realize that in the majority of cases, you do not get in your current financial situation by accident, but rather by virtue of your own actions and decisions about money over an extended period of time.

It's not that your job doesn't pay enough, it's that you have not found a job that pays you more. It's not that your mortgage payment is too high, it's that you bought a house that was too expensive. It's not that after you pay the bills there's nothing left, it's that you spend too much.

This requires a fundamental change in attitude that will be essential if you are ever to successfully apply the principles in this book. You have the ability to change your situation, but you must first realize what your situation actually is.

In most cases, it starts with just rethinking the unnecessary complexity that you have added over the years. Many people simply give into and accept perpetual uncertainty because they have made things so complex that they can't figure out how to change them.

(Setting the Wheels of Change in Motion)

How do you begin? Well, I have already said that I don't believe in detailed financial plans, and I like budgets even less. Many traditional financial thinkers would tell you that these are the two most fundamental steps that must be taken to fix a personal financial problem. Detailed financial plans and budgets only complicate your life and can add frustration and disappointment to what you perceive to be an already discouraging situation.

As you now know, it is my conviction that most personal financial goals can be accomplished with a little common sense, some self-discipline, an appreciation and understanding of the emotional and psychological consequences of your actions, and very little detailed thought or analysis.

Furthermore, those financial goals that seem to require the most analysis to achieve are generally those that incorporate the most uncertainty and speculation about the future. In those instances, a little well-focused analysis will probably end up being equal to or better than an extensive detailed plan.

(Reward Yourself)

Do you remember Pavlov's dogs? They were the ones that were conditioned to perform certain tasks when faced with the prospect of reward. One of the fundamental principles of this research was that the more immediate the reward, the more responsive the dog would be the next time when asked to perform a task. I am not suggesting that people are the equivalent of dogs, but it's simply human nature, as well as canine nature, to respond positively when reward is more immediate. Pavlov's principle is equally applicable to matters of personal finance.

Set goals that are reasonably achievable in a relatively short period of time. Think about retirement planning for example. It's pretty difficult to get too excited about the money you are putting way for something that may not be occurring for years in the future. Instead, focus on something more immediate.

(Targeting Success)

Most people force themselves to take action with their finances when they reach a point where they can no longer tolerate the negative feelings about their current situation.

Problem is, they try to get from point A to point Z without stopping in between to assure themselves that they are headed in the right direction.

Give yourself some things to aim for along the way. Set a series of tangible, achievable objectives to help you build the confidence that you need to go even farther but try not to make your goals unattainable. Setting out an overly detailed financial plan, instituting a meticulous budget, establishing unrealistic spending limitations, and aiming toward lofty financial goals can be just as ineffective a way to achieve your financial goals as having no plans at all.

Channel the discontentment you have with your situation into actions geared toward hitting specific targets. Stop focusing on everything that's wrong and start focusing on specific things that can be corrected. Never be without a target directly ahead of you that you can clearly see. The more targets you hit, the more focused and confident you will become.

(Target Practice)

Here are examples of good and bad targets that you can set:

Bad: I need to make more money.
Good: I need to get my resume updated so I can start looking for a new job that pays more.

Bad: We need to save more money for retirement.
Good: We need to increase contributions to our 401(k) plan.

Bad: We need a bigger house.
Good: We need to save money for a down payment on a new house.

Bad: We need to reduce our debt.
Good: We need to pay off our high-interest department store credit cards.

It is basically a change in philosophy. Take pride when you hit one and move to the next.

(Avoid the Traps)

It's easy to get depressed and frustrated when it comes to personal finances, to give up and feel hopeless and overwhelmed. Unfortunately, many things that traditional financial thinkers would have you do can add to these feelings and emotions, confusing you and pointing out inadequacies that make it even more difficult to achieve your goals and objectives. You must give yourself a chance to be successful.

Changing your personal financial situation is like going on a diet. Unless you really want to make things different, you will inevitably fail. People who are overweight will usually not be successful dieting unless they have become exasperated enough by the situation to motivate themselves into action. The negative emotions are channeled into positive change.

In addition, unless they see tangible results, they just won't be satisfied going from cheeseburgers and tacos to salads and veggies and will likely give up. Stop the comparisons to others. Change your focus from "how much farther do I have to go" to "look how far I have already come."

Can you change the world? Probably not, but you certainly have the ability to change your little piece of it.

Epilogue:
The Power of the Principles

There you have it, the basic principles of simplistic personal finances. Now you have a decision to make. You can finish the remaining paragraphs of this book, close it up, put it on a shelf, and forget you ever read it, or you can take these principles and do something with them.

What you ultimately decide will most likely depend upon how happy or unhappy you are with your current situation. I feel fairly confident, however, that because you took the initiative to acquire this book and since you have made it this far, the concepts of simplicity will not be wasted on you.

Chances are that you have varying opinions about the usefulness of what you have read. Hopefully, some principles struck you as being logical, common sense based, good ideas. Others probably did not elicit such a positive reaction. Before you began, I warned you that much of what you were about to read would defy conventional wisdom and be in direct opposition not only to the way you have become accustomed to doing things but also to what you have been told is the right way.

It's not that my principles represent radical departures from mainstream thinking. Don't be concerned. If you decide to apply any or all of what I have suggested, you will not be considered a financial outcast. You won't be asked to surrender your bank accounts, credit cards, cell phones and computers. These principles were written to address the issues we face given the realities of the modern society we live in and not based upon a desire to or an expectation that we can change those realities.

Believe me, I know we cannot turn back the clock. We must accept our modern society, complete with all its danger, complex technology, overdone analysis and insatiable appetite for information. I just happen to be of the belief that most people, including myself, unnecessarily carry these complexities into our personal financial lives. We have become so accustomed to things being complicated that we tend to think anything that is easy is not worthwhile, and that to be worthy, things must be complex.

(Unconventional Principles)

Skeptics will say that the principles I am promoting are useful only to those willing to accept mediocrity or less than the best. Nothing could be more inaccurate. Remember, the principles are designed to help you identify and push into the background those unimportant things in life that occupy so much of our time and take away from the things that should be most important to us. They are designed to help you change the very way you think about personal financial decisions, focusing less on the pure economic impact of a decision and more on the emotional consequences and practical realities.

There is absolutely nothing wrong with wanting to earn the highest yield possible on your investments, pay the lowest rate possible when borrowing money, minimizing your tax burden, or trying to carefully track where and how you spend your money. Where it all can go terribly wrong is when you are constantly trying to achieve the absolute highest return, the lowest interest rate, the smallest tax bill, and the most detailed analysis of your spending possible. The investment of time and energy necessary to attain these goals often cannot be justified based upon the results. Sometimes you just have to ask yourself if it's really worth it.

It's very easy to get caught up in the complexities of the modern world, especially when it comes to money. Gradually we take steps that move ourselves, oftentimes unnoticed, farther and farther away from the concepts of simplicity. I am suggesting that all of us can learn that just because something is more complex doesn't automatically mean it's any better.

Promoting the concepts of simplicity and stressing the importance of emotion, these principles, when used properly, will challenge you to stop and consider the consequences of each and every financial conclusion you reach before taking action.

Financial complexity is not something that exists independently but is created over time, through a series of seemingly innocent and unrelated decisions. Follow these principles and you will begin to see how these decisions, both major and minor, cumulatively may change your entire life. You will soon realize that the basic concepts of simplicity can be applied to virtually every financial situation and some personal ones as well.

(Sweating the Details)

There are those who have suggested that we need to ignore the small details and focus only on the major things that affect our lives. This is good advice to be sure, and in fact, many of my principles try to get you to do just that.

The only way for most folks to really change their focus away from the insignificant, everyday issues is to minimize the number of details with which they must concern themselves. That is, if you want to concentrate only on those things in life that are truly important, then work to eliminate the unimportant diversions that occupy so much of your time and exhaust your energy.

If you are walking down the street and notice a stone in your shoe, what happens? Most likely you begin to become preoccupied with the irritation. If the stone is large enough or in your shoe for a long enough period, eventually you will be unable to think about anything else. One tiny, insignificant stone becomes your primary focus, and you lose interest in everything else.

The principles help you find those little stones and take them out of your shoe. Rather than telling you not to think about all the details that occupy your everyday life, I suggest that you need to eliminate them. Give yourself a chance to focus on those things that can really make a difference. The principles will help you do that.

(Building Momentum)

Once you begin to understand the principles and start putting them into action, the impact can be dramatic. I want you to start by going back to look again at your complexity quotient from the beginning of the book. It should now be fairly clear to you why I asked the questions that I did. Next, go back and review each principle again and ask yourself honestly, can I apply what is here to reduce my complex number?

You may start out with something as simple as getting all your important papers filed. Then maybe you will take an objective look at how many credit cards you have and, more importantly, need. As you begin to see the opportunities to make things easier, momentum will build. Perhaps you will reconsider your investment strategies or your retirement goals. Maybe you will stop senseless and time-consuming budget analysis or begin to realize the impact of emotional spending and learn to control it. Each principle leads you down a path of understanding. It helps you not only to identify opportunities for simplification but also gives you the knowledge you need to steer clear of the inherent complexities.

Gradually you will begin changing your focus, spending less and less time on the details. You will learn to compensate for perhaps previously unrecognized emotional factors that unwittingly complicate your everyday decisions. As your confidence builds, it will become apparent to you how the concepts of simplicity can be applied to virtually any situation. From relationships to your job, you will find yourself looking for ways to make and keep matters simple. For as simple as the concepts may be, do not underestimate the power of these principles. Soon you find that you have successfully pushed to the background so much of what used to be front and center. All you have left to deal with is the important things in life.

(What I Have Learned)

I could never have imagined when I started writing this book the profound changes that were going to occur in America before it would be finished. This is not the same world it was back then, and it will probably never be that way ever again.

If there is one thing I have learned during my stay on this planet, it's that you cannot live in the past any more than you can in the future. To do so is at best uncomfortable and at worst dangerous. Can we learn from the past? Certainly there are lessons that should not be ignored. Can we make change in response to what we have learned? Definitely we should.

We cannot, however, let the past consume us, especially the negative aspects of it. To do so will suck all of the energy out of today, leaving us lifeless with no hope or confidence in the future.

As I sit here at the keyboard, I must admit having somewhat mixed emotions about coming to the end of this project. It has been more difficult than I could have ever imagined writing a book would be. That being said, I'm going to miss the process.

Sure I will have a chance to catch up on hours of lost sleep and be able to sit down and watch a movie without feeling guilty, but it feels as if I am saying goodbye to a good friend for the last time. Now that it's done, I admit feeling an incredible sense of accomplishment but a little sadness as well.

I have thought about this book often lately, wondering if what I have to say might actually impact someone's life. Somewhere along the way, I have come to the realization that although what I have written may not be all that important in the grand scheme of things, it can make a difference. The message is relevant and important.

You see, the concepts embodied within this book have changed my life for the better. It is a difficult world we live in, but at least I have taken some steps to try and ensure that our tomorrow has a chance of being better than yesterday or today.

Let me assure you, change does not come easily. But if I had not taken action to apply these principles, I would still be preoccupied with all the little things I had allowed to fill my days and my mind. There would not have been much opportunity for progress.

Like most people, I let the talents I was blessed with become hidden behind the facade of what I had allowed myself to become. It's just so easy to keep doing what you are doing, day after day, year after year. Before you know it, life has passed you by and you have done only a fraction, if any, of what you really wanted to do.

You must find some reason in your life to initiate change. Just after the birth of our daughter, I simply convinced myself that life had to be and *could be* much better. Eventually I was able to change my focus and occupy my time pursuing not trivial details but things that had the potential to really make a difference.

The final chapter of this book has yet to be written. It's a personal journey that is not yet complete. Good luck, for it is now time for you to begin your trip down the road of simplicity.

Appendix:
Helpful Web Sites

Please visit us at www.theunfinancialplanner.com

Banking and Internet-Banking Services

www.us.hsbc.com

Cars and Car Safety

www.autobytel.com

www.cars.com

www.edmunds.com

www.hwysafety.com

College Shopping and Savings

www.collegesavings.org

www.fidelity.com

www.scholarships101.com

www.usnews.com

Credit Card Research and Selection

www.cardweb.com

Financial Planning Accreditation Programs

www.aicpa.org

www.fpanet.org

Insurance

www.insurance.com

www.quotesmith.com

Mortgage and Home Equity Loans

www.e-loan.com

www.lendingtree.com

Online Brokerage

www.brokerage.us.hsbc.com

Retirement Savings

www.smartmoney.com

www.vanguard.com

www.401k.com

Stock and Mutual Fund Research

www.cbsmarketwatch.com

www.smartmoney.com